Soul Pirate Handbook

A Devotional for the Good Life

By Luke Lang

Presented to: Lilly Rq

Presented from: Hope Youth Chruch

Date: 6/16/22

THE
YOUTH CARTEL

Soul Pirate Handbook

Copyright © 2016 by Luke Lang

Publisher: Mark Oestreicher
Managing Editor: Tamara Rice
Cover Design: Adam McLane
Layout: Marilee R. Pankratz
Creative Director: Captain Morgan

All Scripture quotations, unless otherwise indicated, are taken from the Holy Bible, New International Version®, NIV®. Copyright ©1973, 1978, 1984, 2011 by Biblica, Inc.™ Used by permission of Zondervan. All rights reserved worldwide. www.zondervan.com The "NIV" and "New International Version" are trademarks registered in the United States Patent and Trademark Office by Biblica, Inc.™

Scripture quotations marked (NLT) are taken from the Holy Bible, New Living Translation, copyright © 1996, 2004, 2007 by Tyndale House Foundation. Used by permission of Tyndale House Publishers, Inc., Carol Stream, Illinois 60188. All rights reserved.

Scripture quotations market (The Voice) taken from The Voice™. Copyright © 2008 by Ecclesia Bible Society. Used by permission. All rights reserved.

ISBN-10: 1-942145-21-7
ISBN-13: 978-1-942145-21-9

The Youth Cartel, LLC
www.theyouthcartel.com
Email: info@theyouthcartel.com
Born in San Diego
Printed in the U.S.A.

For Diana, the Queen of my Pirate Heart...

The Manifest

Freedom

Friendship

Fortune

"Some went off to sea in ships, plying the trade routes of the world. They, too, observed the Lord's power in action, his impressive works on the deepest seas."

— Psalm 107:23-24 (NLT)

"Now and then we had the hope that if we lived and were good, God would permit us to be pirates."

— Mark Twain

Piratical Words Ye Need to Know...

Aft: Short for "after"; toward the rear of the ship.

Ahoy!: "Hello!" or "Hey!"

Arrr!: (Not to be confused with *arrrgh*.) Can mean "yes," "I agree," or "I'm happy." Pirates say this a lot to indicate general approval, but it doesn't mean anything, just keep saying it and you'll be speakin' like a pirate—*arrr!*

Asunder: Torn into different parts; pulled or blown apart in different directions. "The Hull of me ship be blown asunder aft the direct hit o' that cannonball."

Avast!: Derived from "hold fast," which is to stop and pay attention. Has multiple meanings: "Whoa! Get a load of that!" "Check it out" or "No way!"

Aye!: To affirm. "Why yes, I agree most heartily with everything you just said or did."

Aye-aye!: "I REALLY agree!"

Belay: To immediately cease or stop; usually used in disgusted context such as, "Belay that landlubber talk!"

Bilge!: Nonsense or foolish talk. The bilges of a ship are the lowest parts, inside the hull along the keel. They fill with stinking bilge water—or just bilge.

Blimey!: An exclamation of surprise.

Booty: Loot or treasure.

Buccaneer: A general term for the Caribbean pirates.

Cap'n: Short for "captain." As in Cap'n Crunch.

Colors: The Pirate flag, with many variations. (See also, "Hoist the Colors!")

Corsair: A more romantic term for pirate, but still a pirate.

Crow's Nest: A small platform, sometimes enclosed, near the top of a mast, where a lookout could have a better view when watching for sails or for land.

Cutlass: A curved sword, like a saber but heavier; traditional pirate weapon.

Doubloon: A Spanish gold coin. At different times, it was worth either four or sixteen silver pesos or "pieces of eight."

Fair winds!: "Goodbye, good luck!"

Fire in the Hole: A warning before cannon fire.

Fore: Front end of a pirate's ship—or any other ship; short for "forward."

Galley: A ship's kitchen.

Godspeed!: "Goodbye, good luck!"

Grub: Food.

Hearties or Mateys: Shipmates or friends.

Hoist the Colors!: To raise the pirate flag before attacking. Also, a rallying cry for pirates before they go into battle.

Landlubber / Lubber: A non-sailor.

Me: A piratical way to say "my"; as in, "That's me grub on that plate."

No Quarter!: Surrender will not be accepted.

Piece of Eight: Money.

Piratical: Of, or having to do with, piracy and pirates.

Poop Deck: Highest deck at the aft end of a large ship. It has nothing to do with toilets, so don't get any weird ideas.

Savvy?: Meaning, "Okay?" or "Do you understand?"

Sea Dog: An experienced pirate.

Shanty: A sea song.

Shiver Me Timbers!: An expression of surprise or strong emotion.

Thar: The opposite of "here."

Yo-Ho-Ho: Pirate laughter. A very piratical thing to say, whether it actually means anything or not.

AHOY, MATEYS!

Growing up I had a thirst for adventure.
I wanted to live large and loud.
I had an overactive imagination and an allergy to conformity.
We lived out in the country, and we didn't have a lot of stuff.
I learned that doesn't matter.

I looked for danger and excitement in my back yard, and I
found all of the adventure that my imagination could ignite.
I turned sticks into swords and empty cardboard paper towel
rolls into knives. I frantically jumped around, whilst fighting
invisible foes. It's probably a really good thing that we didn't
have close neighbors. I dreamed of taking off and sailing
the deep blue sea. (That's a bit of a challenge when you're
growing up in Oklahoma.)

I wanted to be a pirate.

I would wrap my dad's (hopefully clean) handkerchief around
my head, wear a homemade eye patch and one of my mom's
gaudy clip-on ear rings.

Oh, man! I wanted to be a pirate.

My cousins and I dug hundreds of holes in my grandparents'
yard, looking for or burying treasure. (Fortunately, our
grandparents were patient people who encouraged a little
reckless fortune hunting).

I wanted a life bigger than me.
I wanted to sail away and discover treasure.
For the love of all things, I REALLY wanted to be a pirate.

C'mon, admit it…there's something cool about being a pirate!

Maybe I should clarify…
I'm not talking about the sketchy pirates who go around
stealing, burning things, and being generally antisocial.

I'm talking about a totally different kind of a pirate.
In fact, I want to completely redefine the word *pirate*.
I know that it might seem a little farfetched. But be patient and it will hopefully make sense.

It's not about the looting and lying and belching. (Okay, maybe the belching…put this book down right now and belch like a pirate!)
I'm talking about the sense of adventure (and the questionable fashion sense).
Pirates grow crazy facial hair (even the girls); they wear blousy shirts (even the men); and they proudly sport vests and big earrings, eye patches and cool, pointy hats. They break all of the fashion rules.
Pirates don't conform.

They sail the seas and live the adventure.
A pirate isn't interested in a normal life or predictable life.
They want a life that's risky and ridiculous.
They have an all-consuming urge to dig for hidden treasure.
Pirates want to sing a song, fly their flag, and leave their mark. (C'mon, doesn't that sound like big nautical fun?)
Pirates have their own language. (They said cool, grunty things like *argghh, aye, ahoy*).
They can say the words "poop deck" with a completely straight face.
They even make artificial limbs cool—every pirate wanted a peg leg or a hook for a hand!
They have smart-mouthed parrots perched on their shoulders (which I'm sure is big fun at parties).
They sail the sea to exotic locations, live for adventure, and are constantly looking for treasure.
They stick together. They're a band of smelly misfits who are loyal to each other.
They sing shanties about faraway places and dance to accordion music.
They're stout hearted men and women who live large and free.

I wanted to be a pirate. (I think that I've already made that pretty clear.)

Well, I STILL want to be a pirate.

I'm fascinated with all things piratical. So, a while back I did extensive, grueling research. (I watched movies, read a few books, and even want to an actual pirate museum.) As I studied the life of the pirate, it struck me that most people became pirates because of three main things...

The Freedom
The Friendship
The Fortune

Here's the crazy thing: YOU are probably looking for the same three things. We all spend our lives in search of freedom, friendship, and fortune. The really good news is that I have discovered where you can find them. Interested?

Freedom, friendship, and fortune can be yours. But you're going to have to unleash your inner Soul Pirate.

We all want to be a part of a great adventure.
We REALLY aren't designed to be normal, average, or boring.
We are created to live in the unpredictable wildness of an untamed life.
We are wired for adventure...

We were born to be Soul Pirates.

The Golden Age of Soul Piracy started over 2,000 years ago when Jesus Christ came to this planet and revealed himself to be the Soul Pirate King. He set out on an epic journey. He put out an open invitation to join his crew. He is looking for Soul Pirates.

A Soul Pirate is simply someone who joins in the great BIG crazy adventure of knowing and following Jesus and joins him in plundering hell to populate heaven.

Soul Pirates are spiritual swashbucklers who are honest about who they are and the fact that they aren't meant to sail alone.

Soul Pirates hoist their colors, declare their allegiance, and live knowing that they need a captain. They need to be part of a crew.

Soul Pirates have discovered a love that is deeper than an ocean and a treasure that is worth living and dying for.

Soul Pirates know in their guts that they were not created to conform or hang out in the kiddie pool.

**They have met the Captain of their souls
and are committed to being *themselves* for HIM,
even when no one understands.**

They are committed to going deep into the incomparable richness of relationship with the Soul Pirate King.

So, *arrrghhh!*
Brace yourself and pull up your pirate pants.
We are about to learn from The Captain of our souls and his original little band of misfits about being Soul Pirates.

Jesus had his own special little motley crew; they were fishermen, tax collectors, and freedom fighters...ordinary people with no special training. They were a burly bunch with more guts than manners.
They were more authentic than appropriate.
They were the original Soul Pirates.

We can learn much from the Soul Pirate King about true freedom, real friendship, and lasting fortune.

**Avast, me hearties!
Come aboard and set sail.
It's what you were born for.**

Freedom

"Why join the navy if you can be a pirate?"
– Steve Jobs

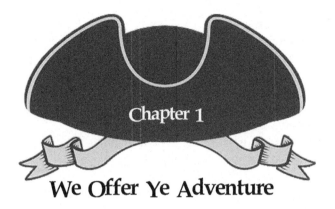

Chapter 1

We Offer Ye Adventure

We want adventure.
We want thrills and excitement.
That's one of the reasons we go to amusement parks.
Melancholy parks never really caught on. Nobody wants to be bored. Nobody wants to be boring.
So, we go to amusement parks and we ride thrill rides.

One of my all-time favorite rides is the Pirate Ship. It is pretty epic.
It looks like a big, beautiful, brightly colored pirate boat, suspended in a sea of freshly paved asphalt. It's not a complicated ride; it simply swings you back and forth. But it's fun!

You get in and the metal bar closes down on you. It takes you backwards to the top, where you sit still for a nanosecond. Then you take a plunge. You are, briefly, separated from your stomach. It is big, exciting, slightly nauseating fun!
Even though there is a bar that keeps you from flying out, it feels wide open. It's freedom! There is a moment when your butt leaves the seat and you are suspended in midair and you

feel totally out of control.

And. That. Is. Crazy. Fun.
There is an element of adventure that you never experience
until you are out of control.

We want Freedom.
Our souls thirst for it.
We crave new adventures, bigger stories.
We don't want to just survive, we want to live.
We want to live authentic...real...raw.
We want to sing songs and tell stories.
**We want to be the wildest, most undiluted version of
ourselves.**

The cure for boring is to go exploring.
We are going to have to lose control.
It's not about safety, it's about significance.Here's what that
adventure looked like in the beginning. Interestingly enough,
it started with some guys on a boat...

> **"One day as Jesus was walking along the shore of
> the Sea of Galilee, he saw Simon and his brother
> Andrew throwing a net into the water, for they
> fished for a living. Jesus called out to them,
> 'Come, follow me, and I will show you how to fish
> for people!' And they left their nets at once and
> followed him. A little farther up the shore Jesus saw
> Zebedee's sons, James and John, in a boat repairing
> their nets. He called them at once, and they also
> followed him, leaving their father, Zebedee, in the
> boat with the hired men."**
> **– Mark 1:16-20 (NLT)**

The Soul Pirate King offered some brothers a simple invitation:
"Follow me, leave what you know. Leave what you can control
and let's take a trip. Join my crew and the world will never be
the same. You will still be fishing for a living, I'm just showing
you a completely new way to do it."

Jesus wasn't asking them to change who they were, he was just asking them to give control of who they were to him.
"Be yourself for me!"
They got out of the boat and followed the Captain.
They gave him control and they found the adventure of their lives.
They had to step out of the certain into the unknown.
They had to step out of the predictable into the unseen.
Faith is going into the deep end.
It is going way over your head, where you could get swept away any minute.
And you're okay with that because you trust the one who is asking you to go deep.

The Soul Pirate King is putting together a crew.
He invites these two sets of siblings to go deep with him.
They trusted the Captain even though they really had no idea who he was.
They joined the crew and started a movement…a pirate party.

Now, it's our turn! Jesus has extended the invitation to come aboard to…well…everybody.
The Soul Pirate King offers us the adventure of a lifetime, the adventure of our lifetime!
It's the same simple invite: "Follow me."

You don't have to have any particular set of skills. You don't have to be pretty or polished. In fact, the qualifications to be a Soul Pirate are that you are strangely unqualified.

> **"The members of the council were amazed when they saw the boldness of Peter and John, for they could see that they were ordinary men with no special training in the Scriptures. They also recognized them as men who had been with Jesus."**
> **– Acts 4:13 (NLT)**

It's all about who we know.
If we know the Soul Pirate King, we can be free.

Soul Pirate Handbook

But to really live the adventure as it is designed, we have to relinquish control. We have to lose control of ourselves. We let Jesus lead the way.

Then…
There is a moment when your soul leaves the seat and you are suspended in midair and you feel totally out of control.

And. That. Is. Crazy. Fun.
And the Soul Pirate King has you the whole time, just like the amusement park pirate ship. There is a bar that holds you at your craziest, uncontrollable moment.

The Soul Pirate King has invited us to trade our lives of comfort and predictability for lives of reckless adventure.

Go deep…
Go over your head…
Lose control.

Let's set a course for adventure...

Set Sail...

- What is the biggest adventure that you have ever experienced? (Amusement park, rock-climbing, drinking expired chocolate milk?)
- What would be your dream adventure?
- How hard is it for you to give control of what you can see to a God who you can't see?
- Why is it important to trust the Pirate King when he asks you to give him control and step into the big unknown?

Think on This Soul Piratical Statement

There is an element of adventure that you will never experience until you are out of control.

Setting Sail for the VAST Unknown

Or "If Grace Is an Ocean, a Soul Pirate Will Do a Belly Flop"

All of my life, I have been mesmerized by the ocean.
Something about the largeness of the sea resonates with the smallness of me.
It calls me into the deep.

Maybe John F. Kennedy was onto something when he said:

> "All of us have in our veins the exact same percentage of salt in our blood that exists in the ocean, and, therefore, we have salt in our blood, in our sweat, in our tears. We are tied to the ocean. And when we go back to the sea— whether it is to sail or to watch it—we are going back from whence we came."

I was on a cruise a while back; we were sailing for the Bahamas. I was sitting in a deck chair facing the ocean, and I just got lost. There was something downright special about the view...
I saw my toes and the ocean.

These are both breathtaking things in their own special way...

the ocean in its beauty and my toes in their ugliness. My feet are like a car wreck. People are repulsed, yet they can't turn away. My toes look like hairy little tater tots, I'm not proud of that. It's just the truth. It's really okay. I'm convinced that most pirates had ugly feet. That is why they wore boots instead of flip flops.

Anyway...on this cruise, while I was hanging out in a deck chair, God reintroduced me to a really cool word: vast!

It's a great word, it's defined as "very great in size, amount, intensity, extent or range."

I like that!

As I was hanging out on the ocean God deposited the word into my spirit.
And he gave me a great visual. I couldn't see the end of water, it stretched on forever! I was smitten by the deep, and I was reminded what vast looks like.

If something is vast, you can't see the end. It's immeasurable... it's countless and uncontainable...it simply goes on forever!

The ocean can be calm or stormy, but it's always beautiful and breathtaking and vast!

It reminds me of something I read...

> **"Your unfailing love, O LORD, is as vast as the heavens; your faithfulness reaches beyond the clouds."**
>
> **– Psalm 36:5 (NLT)**

God's love is vast!
His thoughts for you are countless.
His love is uncontainable.
The richness of Christ in you and me is immeasurable.
We are meant to get lost in the love!

Soul Pirates aren't big fans of cubicles or closets or boxes in general.
They just don't like spaces that are designed to constrict or restrict.
The natural habitat of the Soul Pirate is the wide open.
It's what they were born for.

We were born to live for something bigger than ourselves.

Consider the *vastness* of Jesus!

We can't comprehend the vastness! There's no way to wrap our brains around it.

It's like a little piece of grass...planted in ground...trying to understand how huge the earth is.

God's love never runs out and is bigger than anything we think might separate us from him.

The bottom line is you can't see the end of God!
Consider the *vastness* of Jesus!
Consider the "*un*vastness" of your problems: They might be huge but they are not vast, they will end. You might be going through some really hard times, I don't discount that. But hope says that our problems aren't here to stay. They will eventually cease.

When we focus on the vastness of God it puts everything else in perspective.

We lose ourselves in the vast.
We belly flop into the goodness and grace of God.

Allow the "*un*vastness" of what is bugging you right now get swallowed up in the vastness of the one who loves you right now! Make it a daily goal, to have your breath taken away by the size of your situation.

Soul Pirate Handbook

Get lost in the love...plunge in.

As I sat on the deck, I noticed across from the ocean was a kiddie pool.
It was shallow, not vast! There were kids splashing around in it. The kiddie pool isn't scary...you can see the bottom. If I stood in it, my tater tot toes would barely get wet.

Spiritually, sometimes we spend all our time in the kiddie pool, when the ocean is right there.

Get out of the shallow, get into the vast!

Soul Pirates aren't meant for the kiddie pool.
If you can see the bottom, you aren't where you're supposed to be.
Go deep, get lost in the love!
Move into the vast...get lost in the love...let it swallow you up.
When you get lost in the love, that's all people can see.

Let the vast take your breath away and swallow you up.

Set Sail...

- What is your favorite thing to do at the ocean, pool, or lake?
- When was the last time you wore floaties in public?
- Take a few minutes and do a depth check: When it comes to your faith, are you hanging out in the kiddie pool or are you going deep?
- God's love is vast, our troubles are limited. We need to daily let our problems get swallowed up by his love. How in the world can we do that?
- When you think about the Pirate King and what he has done in YOUR life, what takes your breath away?

Think on This Soul Piratical Statement

If you can see the bottom, you aren't where you're supposed to be.

Chapter 3

Walk the Plank

Have you ever seen a pirate movie with a scene where someone had to walk the plank?

It's scary stuff!

They were usually blindfolded and forced at knifepoint to jump into the murky, shark-infested waters. It was a deadly diving board where prisoners were forced to walk off a wooden plank hanging over the edge. It was a definite departure.
They were leaving behind the boat and taking a plunge into the unknown.

Being a Soul Pirate is all about walking the plank. But it's not what you think! Walking the Soul Pirate plank leads to life and not death.

But it's still pretty scary stuff!

Avast ye! Being a Soul Pirate is a lifestyle of surrender, risk, and adventure.
Soul Pirates are not content with normal. They want to

Soul Pirate Handbook

live a life of adventure and are willing to do anything for
our Captain/Creator. It won't be easy. There will be tough
conditions, but it will be worth it! Soul Pirates are more
concerned with being authentic than appropriate. They are
much more concerned with just being themselves in service of
the Captain than keeping up appearances or the approval of
others.

It's about plunging into the great unknown.
**It's not about reaching the point of no surrender,
It's about reaching the point of absolute surrender.**

The Soul Captain is putting together a crew.
But wait, I've got to be completely up front with you. Because,
Soul Pirates hate fine print! There's a catch. It's free to follow
the Soul Captain, but it's not cheap.

> **"As they were walking along, someone said to Jesus,
> 'I will follow you wherever you go.'**
>
> **But Jesus replied, 'Foxes have dens to live in, and
> birds have nests, but the Son of Man has no place
> even to lay his head.' He said to another person,
> 'Come, follow me.'**
>
> **The man agreed, but he said, 'Lord, first let me
> return home and bury my father.'**
>
> **But Jesus told him, 'Let the spiritually dead bury
> their own dead! Your duty is to go and preach about
> the Kingdom of God.'**
>
> **Another said, 'Yes, Lord, I will follow you, but first let
> me say good-bye to my family.'**
>
> **But Jesus told him, 'Anyone who puts a hand to the
> plow and then looks back is not fit for the Kingdom
> of God.'"**
>
> **– Luke 9:57-62 (NLT)**

Seems pretty harsh, doesn't it? But as any good pirate quickly learns, you can't live with one foot in the boat and one foot on land. You will split your pants, pull a muscle, and quickly fall into the harbor. You have to choose.
You are going to have to walk the plank.
Walking the plank is leaving the old behind.
It's leaving the predictable in the past.

So c'mon…cross the gangplank…surrender. Don't look back. **The Captain says, "Follow me." Jump in! Spectators don't steer history.** True Soul Pirates innovate and instigate.

Maybe you are holding back because the unknown and the unseen scare you.
Maybe it's insecurity or maybe it's security. Either one can hold you back!

Sometimes in order to walk across the plank, we have to stop acting our age.
We have to reawaken something that society has told us to silence.

We are all born with a sense of adventure and a desire to play. We slowly get that squeezed out of us by the so-called realities of life. We become too cool or practical to dig around in the dirt or have epic sword fights with sticks and empty paper-towel rolls.

Maybe people have told you to stop dreaming and digging for treasure. You've been told to grow up…act cool…get civilized and sophisticated. Get practical and act your age.

The problem is that pirates are impractical by nature.
They very rarely act their age.

Adventure isn't a very practical endeavor, it's too risky.
The Pirate Captain once said that unless people believe like kids they will never really experience the treasure of his Kingdom.

So, avast! Don't listen to the people who would hold you back from getting on the boat. It's time to rediscover the part of you that yearns for wild adventure. **Throw yourself into a life of reckless abandon with the Captain of your heart.**
Walk the plank...go from death to life.

Here's a real simple pirate prayer:
I choose to die to myself and live for God.

Set Sail...

- What is the scariest situation that you've ever found yourself in?
- Has anyone ever told you that you were being "inappropriate"? What does that usually mean?
- What is the difference between *authentic* and *appropriate*?
- What does it mean to walk the plank?
- What are some things that you need to leave behind?

Think on This Soul Piratical Statement

Any good pirate quickly learns, you can't live with one foot in the boat and one foot on land. You will split your pants, pull a muscle, and quickly fall into the harbor. You have to choose.

Chapter 4

Plunder Hell

Pirates plunder.
It's an age old tradition.
The definition of plunder is to take or rob, usually by force.
That's not super fuzzy or family friendly.
In most cases, it is a criminal act.
For the record, we do not condone that.

Plundering is a different endeavor for the Soul Pirate.
Think of plundering as more of a restoration project.
You are taking **back** something that originally belonged to the
Soul Captain.
Actually we are taking back someone.
Once we know and follow the Soul Captain, we join him in his
mission.
Like any respectable pirate, we plunder.

We plunder hell and populate heaven.

A Soul Pirate is someone who joins in the great adventure
of knowing and following Jesus and joins him in plundering
hell to populate heaven. Soul Pirates want to plunder hell—

plunder means to take the goods by force.

One day, Jesus was talking to a crowd about John the Baptist (who was a true Soul Pirate if there ever was one!), and he said:

> **"And from the time John the Baptist began preaching until now, the Kingdom of Heaven has been forcefully advancing, and violent people are attacking it."**
> **– Matthew 11:12 (NLT)**

Plundering hell is taking people back by force.
There's no stronger force than love.
It leaves a mark.

Soul Pirates plunder hell by **sharing the treasure**.
It's all about doing something that pirates spent a lot of time doing: fishing!
Remember, Jesus told his original crew that he would make them fishers of men.

> **"One day as Jesus was preaching on the shore of the Sea of Galilee, great crowds pressed in on him to listen to the word of God. He noticed two empty boats at the water's edge, for the fishermen had left them and were washing their nets. Stepping into one of the boats, Jesus asked Simon, its owner, to push it out into the water. So he sat in the boat and taught the crowds from there.**
>
> **When he had finished speaking, he said to Simon, 'Now go out where it is deeper, and let down your nets to catch some fish.'**
>
> **'Master,' Simon replied, 'we worked hard all last night and didn't catch a thing. But if you say so, I'll let the nets down again.' And this time their nets were so full of fish they began to tear! A shout for help brought their partners in the other boat, and**

soon both boats were filled with fish and on the verge of sinking.

When Simon Peter realized what had happened, he fell to his knees before Jesus and said, 'Oh, Lord, please leave me—I'm too much of a sinner to be around you.' For he was awestruck by the number of fish they had caught, as were the others with him. His partners, James and John, the sons of Zebedee, were also amazed.

Jesus replied to Simon, 'Don't be afraid! From now on you'll be fishing for people!' And as soon as they landed, they left everything and followed Jesus."
– Luke 5:1-11 (NLT)

Fish for people.

We plunder hell by bringing people aboard.
We invite them to be a part of the crew...the pirate party.

We fish.

In the Gospel of Luke, Jesus told a great story comparing the Kingdom of God to a party, and he begins to wrap it up by saying: "Go out into the country lanes and behind the hedges and urge anyone you find to come, so that the house will be full" (Luke 14:23).

> **Go out to the highways and hedges and bring in the complete strangers you find there, until my house is completely full.**

We are told to go out and invite people to be a part of the party.

But sometimes people don't want to come on board because they have encountered some angry, mean, or fake pirates. They think that we're all on the same boat.

Soul Pirate Handbook

Sometimes even we get a little confused.

We think our job is to put people in their place, to spend all of our time telling them what they are doing wrong. It's a little like a fisherman who, instead of actually fishing, spends all of his time shouting about how the fish all smell like, well, *fish*. **Instead of putting people in their place, we need to let people know that there is a place for them.**

Here are some random Soul Piratical thoughts about fishing for people…

Serve instead of shout.
Let love be the loudest thing in your life.
Listen more than you talk—you can learn how people are hurting and offer them a cure.
Earn the right to be heard.
Don't be a jerk. I don't see Jesus ever being a jerk. The only one who never sinned was the least judgmental person ever.
Don't be so angry; don't take yourself so seriously.
People are attracted to joy.
Tell stories of hope.
Remember, the gospel means "good news." Jesus compared the Kingdom to a party, not detention.

There's a time for discomfort and conviction that will lead to life change, but the Holy Spirit is so much better at orchestrating that than we are.

Realize who you are representing: the Creator. His amazing creativity is constantly on display in the beautiful diversity of humanity. It's not about making people conform and look like us. People are different from you…that's by divine design…get over it.

Our job is simply introducing people to our best friend and inviting them to his party.

We fish for friends.
We plunder hell.

Don't call people names…lift up The Name that has the power to save and heal: Jesus.

Let's set sail and make some friends.
Leave the anger at home. Anger and hatred aren't good bait.
Love, humility, and honesty are the best bait ever.

Set Sail...

- Have you ever been fishing? If so, what's the biggest fish that you ever caught?
- What are some things that stop us from plundering hell? How can we get past those things?
- Is it liberating to think of sharing our faith as simply introducing people to our best friend and inviting them to his party?
- Have you seen any soul-fishing fails? What are some really wrong ways to try to plunder hell?

Think on This Soul Piratical Statement

Plundering hell is taking people back by force. There is no stronger force than love. It leaves a mark.

Chapter 5

The Articles

You wouldn't think of pirates as big fans of rules. After all, they *are* pirates, right?

We usually think of pirates as generally unruly people who have the manners of a cranky, nap-deprived four-year-old or a middle-aged rock star. But most pirates understood that freedom doesn't come from ignoring rules.

True freedom comes from paying attention to the right rules, boundaries, and guidelines. Because of that, every ship had its own "articles." They were like a constitution for a boat. They consisted of clearly established rules and principles that each crew member agreed to follow. It was like a code of honor, a code of conduct for governing life on board.

Usually each crew member would swear an oath on the Bible, or if they didn't have a Bible handy, they would use a human skull—I'm not making that up! They were required to swear allegiance to the ship's rules before departure or they weren't allowed on the boat.

Soul Pirate Handbook

The company articles would include things like the division of booty (everyone shared in the treasure) and bedtimes (seriously, on most ships lights out was at eight o'clock). They had to keep their weapons ready for service. There was to be no gambling or fighting on some ships. You never messed with another pirate's stuff. Musicians were given a day off on the Sabbath.
The code usually even included a pirate healthcare plan: If you lost a limb, you got extra treasure.

If you didn't follow the articles you were likely to get marooned on your own little island. (Without sunscreen! Oh, the horror!)

The articles could be quite lengthy.
It could get complicated.
There could be a long list to remember!
I've read some articles that went on for pages about the smallest details.

Pirate articles changed based on the captain—some were real control freaks. Others were a little looser.

As Soul Pirates we also have articles.

They keep us focused. They keep us from going overboard. They keep us from getting marooned.

Fortunately, our Soul Captain made it really simple.
He boiled it down to a very simple code…

One day, the Pirate King is approached by a Pharisee. (The Pharisees were pretty much the opposite of the Soul Pirates; they are bound to make sure that everyone is bound by a long, impossible list of rules. They make it impossible for anyone to get on the boat.) This Pharisee is trying to trap the Pirate King by getting him to say something that will turn the crew against him.

But it backfires...

> **"'Teacher, which is the most important commandment in the law of Moses?'**
>
> **Jesus replied, '"You must love the Lord your God with all your heart, all your soul, and all your mind." This is the first and greatest commandment. A second is equally important: "Love your neighbor as yourself." The entire law and all the demands of the prophets are based on these two commandments.'"**
> **– Matthew 22:36-40 (NLT)**

The pirate King refuses to get trapped; he redefines the articles.
He takes the pages and pages of the law and breaks it all down.
He makes it beautifully simple (and simply beautiful).
He boils it all down to *two* things!
Two things, not hard to remember, but sometimes hard to live out:

1. Love God.
2. Love your neighbor as yourself.

There it is! The Soul Pirate Articles! If we are really doing these two things, it covers everything!

The first and greatest article is love God with everything you got...your heart, soul, mind, and guts.
Love God...get a God crush. When you are crushing on someone, they are all you can think about. You see something and wonder what they would think of that thing. You are obsessed! Get a God crush.

Then, when you *really* love someone, you start loving what they love. (This is why, in my married lifetime, I have watched 4,732 hours of Hallmark movies.)
If you love God, you should love who he loves.

Soul Pirate Handbook

Love your neighbor as yourself. Remember, the neighborhood is vast! Your neighbor is everyone you come in contact with, friend or foe. Love them all.
AND love yourself, not in a weird, ego-driven way, but with a realization that you are a unique, priceless masterpiece created by the Soul Captain to be a part of his crew.

Set Sail...

- What are some rules that have never made sense to you?
- If you could make one rule that everyone on the planet had to follow, what would it be?
- What does it mean to really love God? What does it mean to really love your neighbor?
- How does living by the Soul Pirate articles affect everything in your life?

Think on This Soul Piratical Statement

We can stay seaworthy if we live by The Articles.

Read and sign if you're ready.

The Soul Pirate Articles:

Love God.
Love your neighbor as yourself.
Do this and you will stay afloat.

Sign here: _____

Chapter 6

Swab the Deck

Swab isn't really a pretty word.
It's one of those words that sound more like a sound effect
than an actual thing. But on a pirate ship a "swab" was a big
mop.

As a teenager, I learned how to mop. I was a citizen of the
wonderful world of minimum wage. I worked at a grocery
store, and I spent a lot of time with a mop in my hand. I would
have to swab the unidentified mess on aisle eight. I was a
serious swabber. I worked there for five years and I mopped up
every imaginable food product along with a variety of human
waste products.

It wasn't fun, but it had to be done.

It's the same on a boat.
Every pirate had to swab the deck.
It was a routine thing.
It had to be done.
Somebody had to do it.
The pirate had to grab a mop and clean things up.

Soul Pirate Handbook

It was necessary! You had to keep the boat clean.
Evidently, pirates were very sanitary. They liked a clean ship.
It was also a safety issue: If there was extra salt water on a
deck, it could cause people to slip and get hurt. (Especially
people with peg legs.)

The extra salt water also caused things to get rusty.
In order to keep things clean and shiny, you had to swab the
deck.

We also need to spiritually swab the deck.
We need a routine cleaning of the deck...the soul.
We need to take an honest look at our heart/life/habits/
thoughts/attitudes/actions and make sure we are clean.

To live free we need to keep our souls shiny. Stuff happens,
we make choices that corrupt and clutter. We get dirty; it's
probably going to happen.

The especially good news is that the Soul Captain has made a
way for us to stay soul swabbed:

The Captain's blood is the strongest cleansing agent ever.
It's the only thing that can clean a dirty soul.

The Pirate King made it possible for us to be forgiven for all of
our sin and stupidity. There is a really cool promise that serves
as a life preserver for us...

> **"If we confess our sins to him, he is faithful and**
> **just to forgive us our sins and to cleanse us from all**
> **wickedness."**
> **– 1 John 1:9 (NLT)**

We need to keep our souls clean.
That doesn't come from trying harder or trying to be perfect.
It comes from a routine swabbing.

For me, it's a daily thing.

Here is what it looks like...

This is my messy prayer most days:

My God...
I'm a jerk.
Forgive me.
Fix me.
Fill me.
My God...
I desperately need you.
I am weak, please be strong.
My God...
Thank you.
I love you.

Set Sail...

- When it comes to personal cleanliness, how would you describe your style? Spic and span? Neat freak? Hopeless hoarder? Total slob?
- How can your room become a health hazard if you never clean it?
- How can your soul become a health hazard if you never clean it?
- How do we swab our souls?
- Is soul swabbing a one-time deal?

Think on This Soul Piratical Statement

We need to keep our souls clean. That doesn't come from trying harder or trying to be perfect. It comes from a routine swabbing.

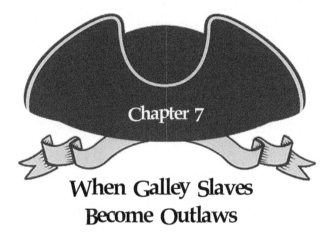

Chapter 7

When Galley Slaves
Become Outlaws

I love stories with big happy endings.

You know, underdog stories where the hero overcomes the unsurmountable odds and wins.

This isn't easy to admit as a burly, hairy-faced dude, but I even love the story of Cinderella. It's perfect! Cinderella, forgotten and left behind, is rescued by a prince, a fairy godmother and—depending on the version—a bunch of singing rodents. She gets to experience happily ever after.

Well, imagine if it all happened on a pirate ship.

Imagine that Cinderella is a galley slave, but one day she is rescued by the Pirate King, and she gets to live out happily ever after as an outlaw.
What? Wait a minute…an outlaw? That's not how the story ends!

Just wait…

Soul Pirate Handbook

On a boat, the galley slave was someone who was, many times, a prisoner of war. They would spend their time chained up in a dark, smelly galley, rowing and rowing and rowing and...you get the idea. There wasn't a lot of opportunity for advancement. It was usually a life sentence, but, because of the conditions, they usually didn't survive long. It was a pretty hopeless situation.

Well, buckle up your boots 'cause I have some bad news for you...

We are born as galley slaves; we are prisoners of a spiritual war.
We are born slaves to two hard, cold taskmasters...sin and death.
It's the law; it's what we deserve. We are slaves.
It was meant to be a life sentence.
It seems pretty hopeless.

But wait...that's not the end of the story.

The ridiculously good news is that we don't have to stay in the galley, the ransom has been paid!

"God's grace has set us free from the law."
– Romans 6:15a (NLT)

Because of the mind-blowing love of the Pirate King, we don't have to be slaves to the law. We can live outside of the thing that would keep us chained up.

Soul Pirates are *outlaws*.

They live *out*side the "law" of this world.
The law of this world would label you and limit you.
It tries to keep you trapped in a prison of condemnation and shame.
But (and this is a huge but), Soul Pirates live as outlaws.
We live as a people who have been rescued *out* of the *law*

of sin and death and made whole, new creatures in Christ.

That is the big happy ending/beginning that we've been looking for.

Set Sail...

- What's your favorite underdog story?
- Before we are rescued by the Pirate King, how are we prisoners of a spiritual war?
- What are some things that enslave us?
- When we live according to the law, we get what we deserve. What are some of the things that we don't deserve, that we experience when we live "outside" the law?

Think on This Soul Piratical Statement

Soul Pirates are *outlaws*. They live outside the "law" of this world. The law of this world would label you and limit you.

Chapter 8

The Black Flag

Flags were a big deal on a boat. You've probably seen one example: the "Jolly Roger," the flag with the skull and crossbones. Flags were a way to communicate between ships, like a pirate emoticon. A white flag signaled surrender to the enemy. A black flag signaled the opposite. It signaled that things were about to get real: "We are at war and we are coming for you."

There's a great big scary world out there and many times we think it's our enemy. We tend to think that other people are our enemies. Especially if we don't agree with them. If they look or think different from us, they must be our enemy, right?

Don't send the black flag up yet.

We were never meant to fight *against* other people, we were meant to fight *for* other people. If you've raised up the black flag against another person or group of people, it's time to bring it down.

Soul Pirate Handbook

But we do have a very real enemy.

You can call him the devil or Satan or the deceiver. In keeping with our lovely little pirate theme, I choose to call him… (dramatic pause)…Darkheart.

The enemy of our hearts is Darkheart.
He is an evil, lying scum. He is a fiend with a heart of the darkest pitch.
He is a sorry puke with a twisted agenda: to steal, kill, and destroy.
He hates the Pirate King, and so he hates what the Pirate King loves. That includes you and that guy that you *thought* was your enemy.

Once we join the crew, we raise black flag and confront the evil one, Darkheart.

We sail into battle with some slightly crazy weapons: our attitude, our faith, our joy. We raise the black flag up, and we go against the enemy with a locker full of weapons that make no sense…no cutlasses or cannons.

One of our weapons is our attitude.

Soul Pirates rebel against Darkheart and his scurvy horde of hate with humility. It really doesn't make sense but the only way for us to be really strong is to get weak.

> **"Humble yourselves before God. Resist the devil, and he will flee from you."**
> **– James 4:7 (NLT)**

Our weakness sets it up for the Pirate King to be strong.
We humble ourselves and realize that we can't do life alone.
We need help. We need the Pirate King to step in and fight for us.

Another unlikely weapon at our disposal is our faith.

That is simply what we choose to believe about God, the world and ourselves.

Faith is not getting it right all the time or not having any doubt.

Faith is choosing God's perspective.

God's word is our double edged cutlass.

Once we have joined the crew, our faith is what Darkheart is trying to snuff out. Without it, it's impossible to please God. This is why Paul (who was one of the greatest Soul Pirates ever) could say with reckless relief at the end of his earth bound journey, "I have fought the good fight. I have finished the race. I have kept the faith" (2 Timothy 4:7).

We'll all finally make it to our finish lines, but the cliffhanger along the way will be this: Will we keep our faith? What's at risk is our active belief in who God says he is, what he says he is like, and what he says he can do.

Another really cool, crazy weapon is joy.

We get to fight back with joy.

> **"...the Joy of the Lord is your strength."**
> **– Nehemiah 8:10b (NLT)**

We have an unseen strength. Even when we face impossibly big problems we can let joy be our weapon, our strength.

Joy is not a feeling or happy little buzz. It's a deep knowing that life may not always be fun or easy, but it's always a gift so I will treat it as such. It's an inner peace that everything is gonna be alright that causes you to rejoice regardless of outward circumstances.

Happiness and Joy are two completely different things.

Happiness is based on circumstances. If everything is going your way...if you are getting what you want...you are happy.

Joy is not about what is happening _to_ you, it's about what happened _in_ you.
Joy is never out of reach, even in the darkest times. Joy is based on the unsinkable fact that God loves you and you can trust him.

So raise the black flag; let the enemy know you aren't afraid.

Set Sail...

- What would your personal pirate flag look like? How would it symbolize who you are?
- What is Darkheart's evil agenda and why is he trying to carry it out?
- What are some ways that you have seen the weapons of attitude, faith and joy used against Darkheart?
- How does being weak set us up to be strong?

Think on This Soul Piratical Statement

We were never meant to fight _against_ other people, we were meant to fight _for_ other people. If you've raised up the black flag against another person or group of people, it's time to bring it down.

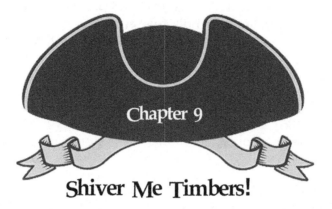

Chapter 9

Shiver Me Timbers!

Some things are meant to be shouted.

"Shiver me timbers" was one of those things.

It should never be whispered or apathetically thrown around.
In pirate stories, "shiver me timbers" was an expression of
excitement or awe.
It is a verbal exclamation point.
It is meant to get attention.

Cap'n Crunch: "**Shiver me timbers!** We are under attack...
someone is hurling giant crunchberries at us!"

It originated from when a wave or cannonball would strike a
ship's mast and send splinters of timber flying. The timbers
would be shivered.

Nothing would ever be the same.

As a Soul Pirate we should have timber-shivering moments.
Our worship should shiver some timbers!

> **"Since we are receiving a Kingdom that is unshakable, let us be thankful and please God by worshiping him with holy fear and awe."**
> **– Hebrews 12:28 (NLT)**

Replace apathy with awe.

Worship should be a timber-shivering experience. It should leave a mark.
We get a really cool picture of that in the story of one Soul Pirate:

> **"Meanwhile, Jesus was in Bethany at the home of Simon, a man who had previously had leprosy. While he was eating, a woman came in with a beautiful alabaster jar of expensive perfume and poured it over his head.**
>
> **The disciples were indignant when they saw this. 'What a waste!' they said. 'It could have been sold for a high price and the money given to the poor.'**
>
> **But Jesus, aware of this, replied, 'Why criticize this woman for doing such a good thing to me?'"**
> **– Matthew 26:6-10 (NLT)**

This woman loved the Pirate King and was in awe of what he had done in her life, so she worshipped him. She poured her expensive perfume on him, and it shivered some timbers.
It made the crew angry.
But it also got the Pirate King's attention.
She was pouring really pricey perfume; it wasn't a loud, huge event. Sometimes timbers get shivered by the smallest expressions of love and awe.
It was brave of this lady. She wasn't worried about price or public opinion.
Timber-shivering worship is courageous and costly.
You want to shiver some timbers? Give away what costs you the most without caring what people think.

Shiver me timbers!!

Set Sail...

- What are some things that should be shouted instead of whispered?
- How would you define worship?
- What are some things that get broke when we shiver timbers with our worship?
- What holds us back from shivering timbers with our worship?
- Why should worship be courageous and costly?

Think on This Soul Piratical Statement

Worship should be a timber-shivering experience. It should leave a mark.

Chapter 10

Give No Quarter
to the Enemy

It's simple really, we give no quarter to the enemy, savvy?

If a ship refused to surrender when they were clearly beat, the other ship would hoist a "no quarter" flag. It had a deep red background and it signified that the winning pirates would now take no prisoners and give no quarter to their enemy.

We have clearly identified our enemy, it's Darkheart.
He has already lost, the Pirate King has kicked his butt. He isn't taking this well, he refuses to surrender to the eternal inevitable. He is still trying to steal, kill, and destroy.

We don't have to give quarter.
We are not letting him take up any space in our lives.
We aren't listening to his lies.
We aren't going to fall for his pathetically uncreative traps.

We refuse to be bullied.
We're not gonna take it.
We aren't letting him sink our ship.
We don't give Darkheart any room or attention.

Soul Pirate Handbook

We can shut him down with our soul swagger.

You read that right, it's all about the swagger. It's long been believed in pirate circles that the more ferocious you look, the less you have to fight. That's why pirates did their best to look intimidating. They were less likely to get challenged if they had a swagger.

Swagger is how one presents him or herself to the world. Swagger is shown from how the person handles a situation. It can also be shown in something as simple as a person's walk. It is confidence and boldness

How can you maintain a Soul Pirate swagger?

How can you let the enemy know that you mean business?

Actually...it's completely backwards from what we normally think of when it comes to swagger: Soul Pirates are actually strongest when they are weak.

> **"So humble yourselves under the mighty power of God, and at the right time he will lift you up in honor. Give all your worries and cares to God, for he cares about you.**
>
> **Stay alert! Watch out for your great enemy, the devil. He prowls around like a roaring lion, looking for someone to devour."**
> **– 1 Peter 5:6-8 (NLT)**

We are raised to assume postures that make us appear strong and independent.
You better strut, be strong and fiercely independent...
swagger.
Never let them see you sweat.

But for the Soul Pirate, the strongest posture is living face down before God.

In Chapter 8 we talked about humility. It's a crazy, soul piratical fact that the most confident thing you can do is be humble. It is meant to show that you are putting your confidence in the right place.

Humility is just being honest about who we are...our strengths *and* our weaknesses.

Then we are honest about who God is.
Then his strengths cover our weaknesses.

Darkheart is strutting around waiting for someone that he can make shark bait.
If we try to live on our own, he will take us down. When we live a life of surrender—give our sins, burdens, worries, strengths, weaknesses, lives to God—we are strong. Soul swagger.

Give no quarter to the enemy...he is beat...don't give an inch.

Be wise. When we strut instead of swagger, we don't hear the enemy sneak.
Climb up into the crow's nest and lookout for the enemy when he slinks in to test you. And surprise him with your swagger.
Humble yourself and let the Pirate King fight for you, he's good at it...

> **"Then Jesus was led by the Spirit into the wilderness to be tempted there by the devil. For forty days and forty nights he fasted and became very hungry. During that time the devil came and said to him, 'If you are the Son of God, tell these stones to become loaves of bread.'**
>
> **But Jesus told him, 'No! The Scriptures say, "People do not live by bread alone, but by every word that comes from the mouth of God."'**
>
> **Then the devil took him to the holy city, Jerusalem, to the highest point of the Temple, and said, 'If you**

are the Son of God, jump off! For the Scriptures say, "He will order his angels to protect you. And they will hold you up with their hands so you won't even hurt your foot on a stone."'

Jesus responded, 'The Scriptures also say, "You must not test the Lord your God."'

Next the devil took him to the peak of a very high mountain and showed him all the kingdoms of the world and their glory. 'I will give it all to you,' he said, 'if you will kneel down and worship me.'

'Get out of here, Satan,' Jesus told him. 'For the Scriptures say, "You must worship the Lord your God and serve only him."'

Then the devil went away, and angels came and took care of Jesus."

– Matthew 4:1-11 (NLT)

Jesus went into this test armed with God's Word and filled with the Holy Spirit and with a serious soul swagger.

We swagger when we know *who* we are, *whose* we are, and we let the Pirate King fight for us.

Set Sail...

- What's the difference between a strut and a swagger?
- How does pride keep us from surrendering?
- How does our culture define and judge swagger?
- How does the Pirate King define swagger?
- How does our swagger become a weapon against darkheart?

Think on This Soul Piratical Statement

We are raised to assume postures that make us appear strong and independent. You better strut, be strong and fiercely independent...swagger. Never let them see you sweat. But for the Soul Pirate, the strongest posture is living face down before God.

Chapter 11

Dead Men
Tell No Tales

There is a common piratical saying that you have probably heard a couple hundred times in movies or theme park rides. It's "Dead men tell no tales." Did you ever think about what it means? Is it that undertakers are really bad storytellers or does it have to do with ventriloquism?

Basically, it means that once a person is dead, they can no longer tell your secrets and stories. Your past can't come back to haunt you through that person. They can't bug you or bring you down. Pirates seem to really like this concept.

Soul Pirates like it too, but in true piratical fashion we twist it up a bit:

Dead men and women live no meaningless stories.

Or, how about this one...

Dead men and women have died to the things that kill and come alive to the things that bring life.

Soul Pirate Handbook

Their past can't haunt them…it died.
Their past stupidity has been dealt with…it was killed.
The Bible puts it like this…

> **"So you also should consider yourselves to be dead to the power of sin and alive to God through Christ Jesus.**
>
> **Do not let sin control the way you live, do not give into sinful desires. Do not let any part of your body become an instrument of evil to serve sin. Instead, give yourselves completely to God, for you were dead, but now you have new life. So use your whole body as an instrument to do what is right for the glory of God. Sin is no longer your master, for you no longer live under the requirements of the law. Instead, you live under the freedom of God's grace."**
> **– Romans 6:11-14 (NLT)**

Consider yourself dead to the stuff that would kill you.
Choose to live a better story, one full of life and hope.
Die to the old ways of living and believing.
Die to sin, don't let it bug you or bring you down.
Give yourself completely to God and he gives you new life completely!

Soul Pirates want to live…really live! To do that you gotta leave the old life behind and set sail on a sea of grace.

Set Sail…

- Pirate ships had some interesting names: the Queen Anne's Revenge, the Black Pearl, the Bachelor's Delight, and the Squawking Parrot. What would you name your ship?
- What does it mean to die to ourselves?
- What are some old ways of thinking that can hold us back?
- How can we live a better story?

Think on This Soul Piratical Statement

Dead men and women have died to the things that kill and come alive to the things that bring life.

Friendship

"Sometimes the most ordinary things could be made extraordinary simply by doing them with the right people."

– Nicholas Sparks

Chapter 12

Picking the Crew

Your crew is crucial.

No one is meant to sail the wide open seas of life and love alone.
You need a Captain *and* a crew.

We can learn *a lot* from the Soul Pirate King and his original little band of misfits about being a crew. In the New Testament book of Matthew, the Soul Pirate King is beginning his epic earth journey, and he does a few things to kick it off. It's like a captain's checklist as he prepares the ship to sail.

In Matthew chapters three and four we read about his soul-seafaring preparations. Jesus is baptized by John the Baptist—*check!* He is given soul provisions from the Holy Spirit—*check!* He is reminded who he is, Beloved of His Father, the Soul Captain—*check!* He fights a fierce battle against the evil Darkheart where he is tempted and tested—*check!* And *then*, he picks a crew...a group of companions for the journey. He makes some friends and invites them to go on an amazing adventure.

Adventure is not a solo sport. Who you chose to sail with is very important.

The Pirate King started picking his crew while he was walking along the seashore, and I have a theory about that. He was walking along the sea, because that's where the pirates are! He knew that if he had a small crew of true Soul Pirates, he could change everything.

Picture this...

> **"One day as Jesus was walking along the shore of the Sea of Galilee, he saw two brothers—Simon, also called Peter, and Andrew—throwing a net into the water, for they fished for a living. Jesus called out to them, 'Come, follow me, and I will show you how to fish for people!' And they left their nets at once and followed him.**
>
> **A little farther up the shore he saw two other brothers, James and John, sitting in a boat with their father, Zebedee, repairing their nets. And he called them to come, too. They immediately followed him, leaving the boat and their father behind."**
> **– Matthew 4:18-22 (NLT)**

He gives them a really simple invitation: COME.

Come, be my friend.
Come on, let's go change the world.

He doesn't promise safety, he promises significance.

He goes on to put together a ragtag crew of spiritually seafaring misfits who left everything behind and followed the Captain.

Here's the ship's roster:

> **"At daybreak he called together all of his disciples
> and chose twelve of them to be apostles. Here are
> their names:
> Simon (whom he named Peter),
> Andrew (Peter's brother),
> James,
> John,
> Philip,
> Bartholomew,
> Matthew,
> Thomas,
> James (son of Alphaeus),
> Simon (who was called the zealot),
> Judas (son of James),
> Judas Iscariot (who later betrayed him)."**
> **– Luke 6:13-16 (NLT)**

This is the original crew roll call. They are a motley crew—
fishermen, tax collectors, freedom fighters. They were ordinary
people with no special training, burly dudes with more guts
than manners. They did inappropriate things, they screwed up,
and they were far from perfect.

They were pirates.

We also know that they were joined by some brave ladies who
didn't let the social rules of the day or their past hold them
back.

> **"Soon afterward Jesus began a tour of the nearby
> towns and villages, preaching and announcing the
> Good News about the Kingdom of God. He took his
> twelve disciples with him, along with some women
> who had been cured of evil spirits and diseases.
> Among them were Mary Magdalene, from whom
> he had cast out seven demons; Joanna, the wife
> of Chuza, Herod's business manager; Susanna; and**

many others who were contributing from their own resources to support Jesus and his disciples."
– Luke 8:1-3 (NLT)

These were women who had been changed because they met the captain. So, they followed him. This was in a culture where women were viewed as second-class sailors. The Captain invited them to be full-fledged crew members, and they got on board. They didn't care what anybody thought. They understood that well-behaved women seldom make history, but pirates do.

They were pirates.

Who you choose as a crew is very important.

It seems that the Pirate King was more interested in authenticity than appearance when he was looking for a crew. He knew that his time was limited, and he was looking for a crew that would steer the ship.

He didn't pick the political.
He didn't pick the perfect.
He picked a bunch of pirates.

That's really good news for those of us who aren't perfect. The Pirate King is still looking for friends to join him on an amazing adventure.
Grab a crew and come on, let's change the world!

Set Sail...

- What makes someone a good friend? What makes someone a bad friend?
- Why is adventure more fun with a friend?
- Why is who you pick as a crew important?
- What does it say to you that the Pirate King was picking imperfect people to be his friends?

Think on This Soul Piratical Statement

Adventure is not a solo sport. Who you chose to sail with is very important.

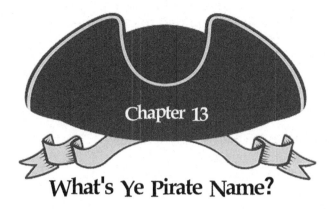

Chapter 13

What's Ye Pirate Name?

Many pirates had actual pirate names. (Shocker, huh?)

Blackbeard is a name that struck fear in the hearts of many people, but his *real* name was Edward Teach, which isn't super intimidating. It sounds more like the name of a pharmacist than a pirate.

John Rackham was called "Calico Jack," because he liked to wear bright, festive colored calico clothing…*totally* true story! He was the world's first fashion pirate!

Henry Avery was called "Long Ben," because he was very tall and because the name "The Dread Pirate Henry" never really caught on.

The same thing happened with the Pirate King's original soul crew.
When they enlisted, it brought a change of identity. The Captain issued new names, new ways of looking at themselves, a new mission.

Soul Pirate Handbook

Simon became "Peter the Rock"!
James and John, the sons of Zebedee, were given the
nickname "The Sons of Thunder" (probably because it's easier
to say than Zebedee).
Jesus gave his closest friends new names...sometimes after
they had messed up. Where we see a weakness he sees a rock.

God is the ultimate pirate name generator.

In my life, I've been called a lot of things.
I've been given many labels.
I've been called some painful names: worthless, good for
nothing, mistake, screw up, too short, too fat, stupid...it's a
long hurtful list.
I've been given labels that can be lethal.
You probably have too.
But, wait. Here's what I've come to realize...
Labels have to be believed to be seen.
People can call you anything and they will.
You don't have to let it stick.

Their labels don't have to become *your* limitations.
If you refuse to believe them, the labels don't stick to your
soul.

Don't let the haters pressure you into being less interesting.
Don't let labels stick.

Labels can be like soul barnacles.
The soul barnacles create soul drag and slow you down.
They can sink your boat.

**If *you* know who *you* are, other people can call you
whatever names they want and it won't change *anything*.**

The only one who gets to define you is the one who made you.

Let the Pirate King tell you who you are!

Some people will try to label you and limit you.
Ignore them.

I refuse to believe the limiting labels. Here is the label that I choose to believe...

> **"...the one who formed you says, 'Do not be afraid, for I have ransomed you. I have called you by name; you are mine.'"**
> **– Isaiah 43:1b (NLT)**

So call me what you want, the truth is that I'm...
Spirit formed...
Empowered by the Holy Spirit…
Rescued…
Ransomed…
Called...
I am his.
These are the labels that I choose to let stick to my soul.
These are my pirate names. (And yours too!)

Ahoy there, rescued and beloved one!
Avast, original and beautiful masterpiece!
Let *those* labels liberate your pirate soul.

Set Sail...

- What is your pirate name?
- What does it mean to you that the only one who gets to define you is the one who made you?
- What are some false labels that others have put on you in the past?
- What are the true names that the Pirate King has given you?

Think on This Soul Piratical Statement

Labels have to be believed to be seen. People can call you anything, and they will. You don't have to let it stick.

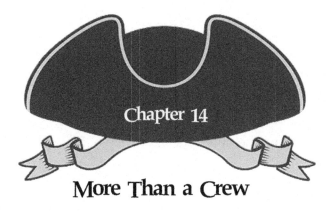

Chapter 14

More Than a Crew

In the old days a lot of orphans and runaways would find their way onto pirate ships. They were lost and alone and they were looking for a crew. They pledged allegiance to The Articles, stepped aboard, and found some mates and more.
They found a place to belong.

It's the same for us. We can find friends that become family.
Belonging is a beautiful thing!

See if you can find the incredible beauty in this verse:

> **"The church sent the delegates to Jerusalem, and they stopped along the way in Phoenicia and Samaria to visit the believers. They told them—much to everyone's joy—that the Gentiles, too, were being converted."**
>
> **– Acts 15:3 (NLT)**

Did you see it?
The beauty of belonging...
It's crucial for the Soul Pirate.

We are misfits, outsiders, and rebels. But we find a place to belong!
We find a crew.

In this verse, the Gentiles (those who weren't Jewish) are outsiders too. They are orphans and runaways.
And now, the outsiders are coming into the crew, and the crew is really happy about it! To the rest of the crew it's a reason to celebrate!
They party when the outsiders find their place…right next to them!

That's the way it should be. It should be a source of uncontainable joy when outsiders become a part of our crew.

A big part of life on a ship was the meal. It was all about the grub and the grog.
It was more of a big family dinner than a formal event. It was a feast with your crew.

Pirates weren't big fans of silverware, it just slowed down the feast. They ate with their fingers and occasionally stopped long enough to wipe the grease from their hands on their beards. (Beards are pirate napkins. For that reason, you should grow one immediately, even if you are a girl. If you can't grow a beard, for whatever reason, you may wipe your greasy hands on the nearest available cat. For more on beards, refer to Chapter 28).

Any time the crew gets together, it really should be like a great big family dinner.
Think about it…
There's nothing like a big sloppy, perfectly imperfect family celebration.

Food…family…fun.
The smells…the sounds…the stories.
At every decent family celebration, there always seems to be that crazy uncle who will, inevitably, say or do something

embarrassing.
It doesn't matter; he still has a place at the table.
There are family members who end up napping in the corner.
There is a cousin who only eats pie.
There is life and laughter.

Church should feel, taste, and smell like a family dinner.
We should share food and drink.
Jesus threw parties where the food never ran out...I like that.
We should share stories.
We should laugh loud and love louder.
Church should smell like home.
There is freedom to be the weird cousin or to take a nap or to
eat a third piece of pie.

We should always be ready to add another leaf to the table.
Everybody has a place.

We *all* get to sit at the kid's table.
We realize that's the funnest place to sit.
You don't have to worry about appropriate.
You can burp and your cousins giggle.
You don't have to worry about which fork to use.
You can turn your fancy napkin into a party hat.
It's a party with your crew.

Everybody belongs.
Everybody has a place at the table!

There shouldn't be any chest-thumping or finger-pointing.
Just hands open in gentle gratitude. The posture of "Whew!
We made it! Pass the green bean casserole!" We celebrate
the beautiful, diverse belonging that we find at the table. **Our
differences make us all the same.**

Let's serve up grace like gravy.
Let's make a place for the outsiders and insiders...
The crazy uncles and hyperactive cousins...
We are family...

Soul Pirate Handbook

A big, crazy, messed-up crew.
You belong here, there's a place for you!

Let's party.

Set Sail...

- Who was the first best friend you can remember?
- Why is it a big deal to belong?
- What is your favorite family meal?
- What is the craziest thing that you ever experienced at a family meal?
- How can we help others belong?

Think on This Soul Piratical Statement

Any time the crew gets together, it really should be like a great big family dinner. Think about it...There's nothing like a big sloppy, perfectly imperfect family celebration.

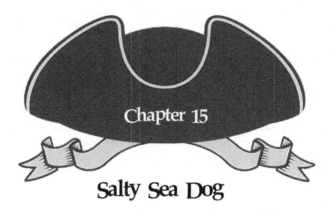

Chapter 15

Salty Sea Dog

Argghh, ye salty sea dog!

Salty sea water is all around the pirate—they taste it, and they smell it.
It floats their boat…literally.
It makes them thirsty for a little grog!

Salt is important.
It brings flavor, it preserves, and it can heal.

The Pirate King told us that we should be salty sea dogs.
What?
We should live to make others thirsty, to bring flavor and to preserve.
We do that by being SEE salt instead of sea salt.

The Pirate King puts it like this:

> **"You are the salt of the earth. But what good is salt if it has lost its flavor? Can you make it salty again?**

It will be thrown out and trampled underfoot as worthless."
– Matthew 5:13 (NLT)

Here's the pirate version of that verse: "Ye are a salty sea dog."

Now, I'm not talking about "salty" the way you might hear it sometimes today—as a slang word for "sassy." You are *not* a "sassy" sea dog! I mean it much more literally. But instead of sea salt (which is amazing on French fries), we should live a life where people can *see salt*!

What are some qualities of salt?
Salt gives flavor, it naturally spices things up!
Salt is a preservative; it keeps things from rotting.

Soul Pirates are supposed to bring flavor to a tasteless world. We should be living with zest...living for God adds spice to life.

"Taste and see that The Lord is good."
– Psalm 34:8a (NLT)

We need to bring the flavor! Soul Pirates should be the most creative, exciting, fun people on the planet.

Boring is safe.

You will be told to behave yourself.
The scolders could have, would have, and should have.
But they didn't and now they resent your adventure.

Ignore them.
Banish the bland!

Salt also has a preserving effect. Some of Jesus's original crew were fishermen. They would pack fish in salt to preserve it, keep it from spoiling and getting funky. Salt would keep it fresh.

Our world is rotting, as salty sea dogs we should be preserving the world around us. Keep it from going totally bad.

Here's the kicker...for salt to work, it has to come into contact! It has to touch what it is flavoring or preserving. It has to come out of the shaker.
As a salty sea dog, you need to learn how to best be salt.

Salt can be used or abused. Too much salt can ruin a meal. Putting it in someone's eyes would be really mean, because it would sting. But the right amount brings out just the right flavor.

Salt is subtle, we don't usually see it, we taste it. It subtly makes a difference. Over time you see its preserving influence. You might not see an immediate difference, but salt instantly changes whatever it touches.

Salt is a subtle, preserving influence that adds zest and flavor. Salty sea dogs are meant to bring the right amount of flavor to a situation.
Do people see salt in us?

Set Sail...

- What is your favorite salty thing to eat?
- What does salt do?
- How can we live as see salt?
- How have you seen sea salt used and abused?

Think on This Soul Piratical Statement

We need to bring the flavor! Soul Pirates should be the most creative, exciting, fun people on the planet.

Chapter 16

Be the Lighthouse

In the seafaring world, lighthouses are pretty important!
They are towers with a bright light on top.

They serve two big purposes:

    1. They serve as a navigational aid.
    2. They warn boats of dangerous areas.

In other words, they help travelers find their way.

Along with being salty sea dogs, the Pirate King tells us that
we need to be…um…lighthouses.
In the soul-seafaring world, it's a pretty important thing!
See the lighthouse…
Be the lighthouse.

We need to help wandering travelers find their way.

Soul Pirate Handbook

The Pirate King puts it like this:

> **"You are the light of the world—like a city on a hilltop that cannot be hidden."**
> **– Matthew 5:14 (NLT)**

Here's the pirate version of that scripture:

> "Ye are a lighthouse to help wandering travelers find their way."

Light dispels and defuses darkness.
Light is always stronger than darkness.
In the darkest night you can always see the smallest light.
We, as Soul Pirates, get to illuminate the path for the people around us.

> **"For once you were full of darkness, but now you have light from the Lord. So live as people of light! For this light within you produces only what is good and right and true."**
> **– Ephesians 5:8-9 (NLT)**

Our influence depends on us being visible.
Don't be surprised that we live in a dark world.
Aside from us they have no source of light. We need to glow!

The crazy thing is that it's not *our* light; we can't generate our own light. It's the light of Christ shining in and through us. Our job is to just let it shine through.
Let your light shine, show the travelers who are stumbling in the dark the way.

So, let's review…we are both salty sea dogs and lighthouses. It's important that we learn how to best be both.

Like salt, light can be used or abused.
If you shine a bright light in someone's eyes, they probably won't appreciate it.

Show them the path and they think you are great.

Different situations call for different approaches.
Sometimes you will be a salty sea dog and sometimes you will
be a lighthouse.
Remember, salt is subtle, we don't usually see it, we taste it.
It subtly makes a difference. Over time you see its preserving
influence.

On the other hand, light is instantly visible. It overtakes
darkness.
They both instantly change whatever they touch.
There are times that you will be more salt than light and vice a
versa.

Salt is a subtle, preserving influence that adds zest and flavor.
Light is a bold influence that instantly penetrates the darkness.

Be the lighthouse!
Help wandering travelers find their way home.

Set Sail...

- Have you ever used a nightlight? (Don't be ashamed!)
  What did the nightlight do for you?
- Why are lighthouses really important to a pirate?
- How can you shine a light on your slice of the world
  today?
- How do we try to hide our light? Why?
- What are the differences between salt and light?

Think on This Soul Piratical Statement

In the darkest night you can always see the smallest light.
We, as Soul Pirates, get to illuminate the path for the people
around us.

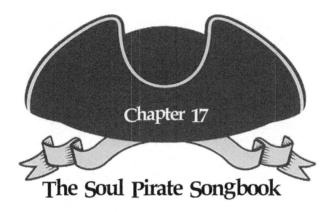

The Soul Pirate Songbook

C'mon sing it with me..."Yo-ho, yo-ho, a pirate's life for me..."
Yup, now that song will be stuck in your head for at least the
next 43 minutes. (You're welcome!)

Every major event on a pirate ship is accompanied by song
or shanty. They would sing songs while they worked to make
time go faster. They were half-sung and half-chanted in a kind
of call and response thing. They were songs of commentary
(about the day or recent events) or songs of conversation,
or songs of celebration about their exploits.

Here is a completely random and totally true fact: In the State
of North Carolina (where I live), there is a crazy state law in the
books. It is against the law to sing off key. Here's my theory
about this law, I think it's due to the large amount of pirates
who lived in North Carolina at one point and their propensity
to loudly sing shanties.

A Soul Pirate doesn't let anything keep them from singing.

Music plays a very important role in the life of a Soul Pirate!

Soul Pirate Handbook

That is why we should have a soul Pirate songbook.

For the Soul Pirate, life is meant to have a lyrical quality.
Sometimes life will be a joyful romp, sometimes it's going to
be a sad shanty, but there will always be a song.
**There should always be sweet music igniting the soul and
moving the feet.**

We sing songs of commentary and conversation and
celebration of the exploits of our Pirate King.

Our songs become prayers, our prayers become songs.

Life is a perpetual song.

> **"...Singing psalms and hymns and spiritual songs
> among yourselves, and making music to the Lord in
> your hearts."**
> **– Ephesians 5:19 (NLT)**

A really good pirate song can shake things up! Look at this
story:

> **"Around midnight Paul and Silas were praying and
> singing hymns to God, and the other prisoners were
> listening. Suddenly, there was a massive earthquake,
> and the prison was shaken to its foundations. All
> the doors immediately flew open, and the chains of
> every prisoner fell off!"**
> **– Acts 16:25-26 (NLT)**

The Soul Pirates, Paul and Silas, are beat up and thrown into
prison.
They are locked up in an unbelievably nasty dungeon.
This could be a little discouraging; it might cause you to forget
the lyrics.

Not these incarcerated individuals, they choose to sing.

When they sing, the earth shakes and their chains are broken.
That is a powerful soul shanty!

There is a great Soul Pirate's songbook in the Old Testament,
it's called the book of Psalms.
It's made up of 150 songs—love songs about hope, thanks,
doubt, fear, and failure.
It's honest, gut-level stuff.
Most of it written by David, a ragtag shepherd boy who
became a Soul Pirate...

Here are some of the songs...

**"O Lord, our Lord, your majestic name fills the
earth! Your glory is higher than the heavens."**
– Psalm 8:1 (NLT)

**"Those who live in the shelter of the Most High
will find rest in the shadow of the Almighty.
This I declare about the Lord:
He alone is my refuge, my place of safety;
he is my God, and I trust him."**
– Psalm 91:1-2 (NLT)

**"Search me, O God, and know my heart;
test me and know my anxious thoughts.
Point out anything in me that offends you,
and lead me along the path of everlasting life."**
– Psalm 139:23-24 (NLT)

**"Let the godly sing for joy to the Lord;
it is fitting for the pure to praise him.
Praise the Lord with melodies on the lyre;
make music for him on the ten-stringed harp.
Sing a new song of praise to him;
play skillfully on the harp, and sing with joy."**
– Psalm 33:1-3 (NLT)

Soul Pirate Handbook

Sing a sweet love song.
Release your heart's joy.
Live out some awe-filled lyrics.
Make some noise!

We are brothers and sisters, united in the understanding that we are misfits in desperate need of a Captain who will rescue us and show us the way. There is no room for faking, pretending, or posturing. We need God, and we need each other.

So, we gather together to sing from the same tattered songbook. We all sing it in our own unique lyrical life stylings.

We are grateful for grace and thankful for freedom.
We are singing the song of the redeemed...I once was lost, but now, I'm found...was blind but now I see.

There's a great song given to us in Philippians 2:6-11.
Read this, or even better sing it...

> **"Though he was God,**
> **he did not think of equality with God**
> **as something to cling to.**
> **Instead, he gave up his divine privileges;**
> **he took the humble position of a slave**
> **and was born as a human being.**
> **When he appeared in human form,**
> **he humbled himself in obedience to God**
> **and died a criminal's death on a cross.**
>
> **Therefore, God elevated him to the place of highest**
> **honor and gave him the name above all other names,**
> **that at the name of Jesus every knee should bow,**
> **in heaven and on earth and under the earth,**
> **and every tongue declare that Jesus Christ is Lord,**
> **to the glory of God the Father."**
> **– Philippians 2:6-11 (NLT)**

Now, go back and try to sing it again as loud as you can!

That's from a letter written by the Dread Pirate Paul, the same guy who busted out of prison with a song. Once he was an arrogant, cold-blooded, religious jerk. Then he met Jesus and became a Soul Pirate. He was chosen by God to love and care for the same people he once tried to murder.
I think he liked to sing.

Sing your own song—it doesn't have to be pretty or perfect or on pitch.
It just needs to be an honest expression of your heart.
Express your love, joy, hope, hurt, thanks, faith, doubt, or anger.
Someday we will join in the ultimate sing-along with a song for the pirate captain.
(Pirates love sing-alongs! In a pirate sing-along, nobody has to sing alone!)

Here's a sneak preview of what that will look like:

> **"Then I looked again, and I heard the voices of thousands and millions of angels around the throne and of the living beings and the elders. And they sang in a mighty chorus:**
>
>> **'Worthy is the Lamb who was slaughtered—
>> to receive power and riches
>> and wisdom and strength
>> and honor and glory and blessing.'**
>
> **And then I heard every creature in heaven and on earth and under the earth and in the sea. They sang:**
>
>> **'Blessing and honor and glory and power
>> belong to the one sitting on the throne
>> and to the Lamb forever and ever.'"**
>> **– Revelation 5:11-13 (NLT)**

Soul Pirate Handbook

Set Sail...

- What's your favorite song of all time?
- What's your favorite musical style?
- How does music make life better?
- What can we learn from Paul and Silas singing in prison?
- Piratical dare: Start a sing-along with a random stranger!

Think on This Soul Piratical Statement

For the Soul Pirate, life is meant to have a lyrical quality. Sometimes life will be a joyful romp, sometimes it's going to be a sad shanty, but there will always be a song. There should always be sweet music igniting the soul and moving the feet.

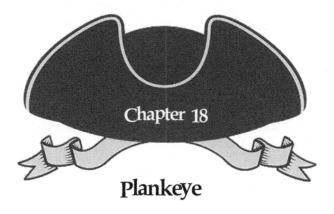

Chapter 18

Plankeye

True story: I'm blind in one eye. This gives me a legal excuse to dress like a pirate; I can wear an eyepatch all the time. I've been blind in my left eye since birth; I have a detached retina.

When I was a little kid, my eye doctor thought I was faking it. For some unbeknown reason, he was convinced I was just being lazy. So he came up with a brilliant, yet really cruel plan: He put an eyepatch on my *good* eye. This was meant to force me to use my bad eye, but it didn't work. It just caused me to walk into walls and fall down a lot. I had to stumble around like this for a couple of weeks. Finally, the evil eye doctor admitted that, *yes*, I was actually blind.

Because of this experience, I learned a valuable piratical life lesson: You gotta wear your eyepatch on the right side! (This, for me, is the left side!)

There's another Soul Pirate eye affliction that is much more serious: *plankeye!*

In a pirate's world, a plank is something that you walk, *not* something that you wear. You especially don't want to wear a plank on your face. That would be unsightly, uncomfortable and downright awkward!

Anytime you are doing life with a crew, things happen and people bug you. You get irritated, and you notice things about others that you don't see in yourself.

When this happens, we can get a disease that seriously impairs our vision: plankeye.

People, the threat of plankeye is real!

And clear vision is a big deal.
So much of faith is about vision...perspective...what we choose to see. Where we choose to focus...seeing the unseen.

The Pirate King warns us about the dangers of plankeye:

> **"And why worry about a speck in your friend's eye when you have a log in your own? How can you think of saying to your friend, 'Let me help you get rid of that speck in your eye,' when you can't see past the log in your own eye? Hypocrite! First get rid of the log in your own eye; then you will see well enough to deal with the speck in your friend's eye."**
> **– Matthew 7:3-5 (NLT)**

The Voice Bible puts it like this: "Don't ignore the wooden plank in your eye, while you criticize the speck of sawdust in your brother's eyelashes...Remove the plank from your own eye, and then perhaps you will be able to see clearly how to help your brother flush out his sawdust."

We can all get planks in our eyes.
They impair our vision.
They keep us from seeing the truth about ourselves and others.

They keep us from believing and being who we were born to be.

Some of our planks are self-inflicted…things like unforgiveness, self-righteousness, jealousy, pride. All of these seriously impair our vision and fry our focus.
We can also get plankeye when someone has poked us in the eye with their words, actions, or betrayal and the plank remains. It's a very real hurt that clouds and colors our world.

Planks can be old ways of doing things or lies that we believe about ourselves or others.

We will never see *anything* clearly with plankeye.
We have to choose to see.
Get the plank out.
Drop whatever is hurting our vision.
Choose to see the unseen.
C'mon…focus!
Fix your eyes on King Jesus so that he can fix your eyes.

We need to see people, situations, hurts, setbacks, and successes through the eyes of Christ, not through the plankeye.
The *world* looks different through the eyes of Christ.
We look different through the eyes of Christ.

Get our eyes off the storms…get our eyes off ourselves…get our eyes off others…get our eyes on the Savior.
When Christ is central, everything else is peripheral.
We need new eyes: his eyes.

A vision transplant is the only cure for plankeye.
It's all about focus.
Fix your eyes on King Jesus, so that he can fix your eyes.
Fix your eyes on King Jesus, so that your eyes don't wander.
Walk the plank, don't wear it!
Adjust your eyepatch and focus on the Pirate King.

Soul Pirate Handbook

Set Sail...

- Why is so much of faith about focus and what we choose to see?
- What are some of the planks that can impair our vision?
- How does fixing our eyes on the Pirate King fix things?

Think on This Soul Piratical Statement

We need to see people, situations, hurts, setbacks, and successes through the eyes of Christ, not through the plankeye.

Chapter 19

Pardon Me, but Is That
Salty Sea Air I Smell?

I love the smell of the sea! It's like a magical elixir for my soul. But to my wife, on the other hand, it smells like fish. What smells like freedom to some people irritates others. It is either fragrant or funky. Some people love the smell of the ocean, to them it smells like sunshine. Some people hate it, to them it smells like dead fish.

It's the same spiritually: What smells like freedom to some people irritates others. The fragrance of Christ is refreshing to some people and convicting to others.

> **"Our lives are a Christ-like fragrance rising up to God. But this fragrance is perceived differently by those who are being saved and by those who are perishing. To those who are perishing, we are a dreadful smell of death and doom. But to those who are being saved, we are a life-giving perfume. And who is adequate for such a task as this?"**
> **– 2 Corinthians 2:15-16 (NLT)**

The way we live smells! It's supposed to.

We should smell like the Pirate King. People should be able to tell that we have been around him simply by the way our life smells. To some people that will be a sweet odor, to others it will be a noxious fume that reminds them they aren't living for the Pirate King.

We do need to check ourselves. If we offend others, we need to make sure we aren't giving off a selfish, stupid stench. We've got to ask ourselves how we smell spiritually—are we fragrant or funky?

We should smell like the Pirate King.
We are the aroma of Christ…the unmistakable scent of fresh hope.

> **"Live a life filled with love, following the example of Christ. He loved us and offered himself as a sacrifice for us, a pleasing aroma to God."**
> **– Ephesians 5:2 (NLT)**

Have you ever hugged someone who was wearing a lot of cologne or perfume and you walk away smelling like that person? Their fragrance has rubbed off on you, and you carry their scent. It comes from contact. That's how it's supposed to be with Christ when we spend time with him. We get as close as we can. We walk away with his scent. He has rubbed off on us. The way we treat others gives off an unmistakable fragrance.

Pardon me, but is that salty sea air I smell?

Set Sail...

- What is your favorite smell?
- What is a smell that really irritates you?
- How do we start to smell like the Pirate King?
- What are some ways that you can give off faith fumes?

Think on This Soul Piratical Statement

We should smell like the Pirate King. People should be able to tell that we have been around him simply by the way our life smells. To some people that will be a sweet odor, to others it will be a noxious fume that reminds them that they aren't living for the Pirate King.

Chapter 20

Hoist the Mainsail!

Here's a little unsolicited nautical information for you: On a boat, the principle sail is called the mainsail. It is the lowest and largest sail on the mast. It steers the boat. It's very important; you aren't really going anywhere without it.

On a pirate ship, at the beginning of a journey, you would hear the order, "Hoist the mainsail!" Hoisting, or raising, the mainsail is one of the first steps in setting sail. Really simply, it makes you move.

As Soul Pirates, compassion should be our mainsail. Compassion should drive the Soul Pirate and keep them on course. It should help us steer past self.

Jesus was steered by compassion.
Even when he didn't feel like it.
When Jesus was on this planet, he was both totally God and totally man.
He had bad days; he got tired.

In Mark 6, he's having a rough time. He has been rejected in his hometown. A friend has been killed and people just won't leave him alone. His crew can't even find the time to eat. So, like any good crew of Soul Pirates, they set off to sea. He just wants to go on a little boat ride with his crew. But compassion is the mainsail for Jesus and it helps him steer past self.

> "They left by boat for a quiet place, where they could be alone. But many people recognized them and saw them leaving, and people from many towns ran ahead along the shore and got there ahead of them. Jesus saw the huge crowd as he stepped from the boat, and he had compassion on them because they were like sheep without a shepherd. So he began teaching them many things.
>
> Late in the afternoon his disciples came to him and said, 'This is a remote place, and it's already getting late. Send the crowds away so they can go to the nearby farms and villages and buy something to eat.'
>
> But Jesus said, 'You feed them.'
>
> 'With what?' they asked. 'We'd have to work for months to earn enough money to buy food for all these people!'
>
> 'How much bread do you have?' he asked. 'Go and find out.'
>
> They came back and reported, 'We have five loaves of bread and two fish.'
>
> Then Jesus told the disciples to have the people sit down in groups on the green grass. So they sat down in groups of fifty or a hundred.
>
> Jesus took the five loaves and two fish, looked up toward heaven, and blessed them. Then, breaking the loaves into pieces, he kept giving the bread to

**the disciples so they could distribute it to the people.
He also divided the fish for everyone to share. They
all ate as much as they wanted, and afterward, the
disciples picked up twelve baskets of leftover bread
and fish. A total of 5,000 men and their families were
fed."**

– Mark 6:32-44 (NLT)

Jesus, the Pirate King, has great compassion for the horde
because they are like "sheep without a shepherd." They are
helpless, hungry and confused. He steers past self and helps
meet their needs. He gives them some navigation and a
miracle sack lunch.

As part of the crew, we should be doing what we see the Pirate
King doing.

**Compassion is our mainsail.
It should set us off in the direction of mercy.**

Compassion should steer us beyond ourselves.
It should cause us to do something. It doesn't have to be a big
something, just something that helps another traveler.
It should set us up for acts of soul piratical kindness.

Any sailor can notice a need, but Soul Pirates do what they can
to meet the need.
Let's be honest, we rarely feel like sailing the extra mile for
someone in need. We get tired, we get busy...
Hoist the mainsail!

It's not convenient, it's hard, it costs us something...
Hoist the mainsail!

Allow compassion to steer you past yourself into the unknown
waters where you can make a difference.
HOIST THE MAINSAIL!

Soul Pirate Handbook

Set Sail...

- What are some things that can steer people through life?
- Why is being steered by compassion a hard concept sometimes?
- When was the last time you remember being moved by compassion?
- What are some acts of soul piratical kindness you can do this week?

Think on This Soul Piratical Statement

Compassion should steer us beyond ourselves. It should cause us to do something. It doesn't have to be a big something, just something that helps another traveler.

Fortune

"There comes a time in every rightly constructed boy's life when he has a raging urge to go somewhere and dig for hidden treasure."

– Mark Twain

Chapter 21

X Marks the Spot?

Here's a highly questionable history lesson for you…
Pirates were all about treasure. They sailed the seas in search
of fortune: rubies, emeralds, diamonds.

But there was a problem. There didn't seem to be any pirate
banks. You can't just put your rubies in an ATM. So they buried
their treasure and would carefully draw a map to show them
how to get back to the booty. They needed something to mark
the exact spot on the map where the treasure could be found.
X became the universally recognized piratical symbol for "the
booty is *right here!*"

Soul Pirates have found the richest treasure ever: knowing
Jesus!

It's found at the X, the cross marks the spot!

We are all born with a thirst for treasure, but not the kind that
can be buried in a box. We long for treasure that can only be
found because of a cross and an empty tomb. It's everlasting
treasure! Eternal treasure that can't be soiled or stolen!

> **"Don't store up treasures here on earth, where moths eat them and rust destroys them, and where thieves break in and steal. Store your treasures in heaven, where moths and rust cannot destroy, and thieves do not break in and steal. Wherever your treasure is, there the desires of your heart will also be."**
>
> **– Matthew 6:19-21 (NLT)**

X marks the spot where we find the richest treasure.

In ancient days, the X was a symbol for Christ. It came from the first letter of the Greek word for Christ. (So when people write Xmas instead of Christmas, it's not disrespectful, it's simply an abbreviation…so chill out!) So…X (or Christ) totally marks the spot where we find soul fortune!

Treasure isn't about doubloons or jewels, it's about knowing and being known by Jesus.

The Soul Pirate adventure begins as we do life with Jesus and make him known to those around us. The Pirate King told a great story to illustrate all of this about a black pearl…

> **"The Kingdom of Heaven is like a treasure that a man discovered hidden in a field. In his excitement, he hid it again and sold everything he owned to get enough money to buy the field.**
>
> **Again, the Kingdom of Heaven is like a merchant on the lookout for choice pearls. When he discovered a pearl of great value, he sold everything he owned and bought it!"**
>
> **– Matthew 13:44-46 (NLT)**

We are spiritual treasure hunters in search of the pearl of great price that changes everything! **The real treasure is living the adventure with the Soul Pirate King.**

Then, in an unexplainable crazy twist, when we find our treasure in him, God puts his treasure in us.
(Read that last sentence again twice)

We become treasure chests!

> **"Don't you realize that your body is the temple of the Holy Spirit, who lives in you and was given to you by God? You do not belong to yourself, for God bought you with a high price. So you must honor God with your body."**
> **– 1 Corinthians 6:19-20 (NLT)**

When we find our treasure in him, the Pirate King puts his treasure in us! He gives us the Holy Spirit.

We contain the greatest treasure! The Holy Spirit has taken up residence in us.

He fuels our adventure and gives us strength for the journey.

You are a box for holy booty!

Ahoy...thar's great treasure in you!

Set Sail...

- In our pursuit of money and stuff, how does the thought that Soul Pirates have found the richest treasure ever—knowing Jesus—change all the rules?
- Draw a picture of your spiritual journey as a treasure map, with X marking the spot where you found and followed the Pirate King.
- As a Soul Pirate, you have the Holy Spirit living in you. That makes you a walking, talking treasure chest. How should that affect your self-image and lifestyle?

Soul Pirate Handbook

Think on This Soul Piratical Statement

We are spiritual treasure hunters in search of the pearl of great price that changes everything! The *real* treasure is living the adventure with the Soul Pirate King.

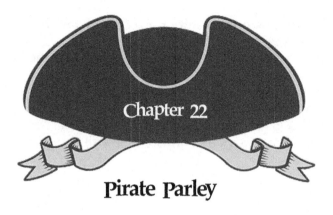

Chapter 22

Pirate Parley

Maybe you've heard the term "pirate parley" from *Pirates of the Caribbean*. Evidently, it was thought up by the French. It is not to be confused with parsley (which is a popular herb). Parley is part of the pirate code. It entitles the invoker with free passage to negotiate with a ship's captain. If a passenger were on board and needed help that only the captain could give, they would invoke parley by saying, "You must take me to your captain."

There is a Soul Pirate parley too:

> **"This High Priest of ours understands our weaknesses, for he faced all of the same testings we do, yet he did not sin. So let us come boldly to the throne of our gracious God. There we will receive his mercy, and we will find grace to help us when we need it most."**
> **– Hebrews 4:15-16 (NLT)**

Because of what the Soul Pirate King did for us we have free passage to God! We can be taken to the Captain! We have immediate access to the throne room of the Eternal One.

**Don't waste this opportunity for an *awe*-filled life
of *awesomeness*.**
It's all about invoking parley and getting access to the Pirate
King.
It's all about getting as close as you can to the Soul
Pirate King.
Lean in! Get in his face.
That is the secret to a life of awesome! It's all about getting
close.

Parley creates proximity, don't waste the opportunity.

Read this verse out loud, preferably in a British accent:

> **"They were now on the way up to Jerusalem, and
> Jesus was walking ahead of them. The disciples were
> filled with awe, and the people following behind
> were overwhelmed with fear."**
> **– Mark 10:32a (NLT)**

Read that verse again (without the accent) and pay attention
to where people were and what they were feeling.

Many people were following Jesus that day, some were filled
with awe and some were overwhelmed with fear...interesting.

What is the difference between fear and awe?
Awe is all about wonder, fear is all about worry.
Awe captivates, it makes you go WOW!
Fear cripples, it makes you go WHOA!

The Soul Pirate life can be a little scary, you don't know what
waits around the bend. But just because it's scary doesn't
mean it has to be fearful.

The disciples were following up close, they were filled with
awe.

The people following at a distance were overwhelmed with fear.
The closer you get to Jesus the more fear is transformed into awe.
If I'm not astonished by Jesus on a daily basis, I'm not close enough.

You can't be caught up in wonder while watching from the back of the boat.
Get close and be amazed by grace!
Lean hard into the Captain.
The way has been made for you to get as close as you want.

Parley creates proximity, don't waste the opportunity.

Set Sail...

- Have you ever been close to a celebrity? What was that like? How did you feel? Were you scared or nervous?
- When it comes to the Pirate King, how do we turn fear into awe?
- Who determines how close you can get to the Pirate King?
- What are some ways to lean into the Pirate King and get as close as we can?

Think on This Soul Piratical Statement

Soul Pirate parley means that we can live right up close to the maker and maintainer of the universe. That's a pretty big deal!

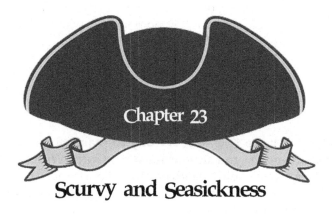

Chapter 23

Scurvy and Seasickness

There were a couple of seriously nasty afflictions that could ruin a pirate's day:
Scurvy—a nasty disease caused by a vitamin deficiency.
Sea sickness—not so much a disease as a dire need to throw up.

Both of these could rock your boat and make you sicker than a parrot that has eaten too much pizza. "*Urp*...Polly wants an antacid!"

They are both also concerns for the Soul Pirate. We can come down with spiritual scurvy and sea sickness of the soul.

How can we be healed from these irritating spiritual afflictions?

What is spiritual scurvy?
Back in the day, scurvy was a nasty disease caused by a vitamin-C deficiency. If pirates didn't eat the right stuff, they would get scurvy which caused them to lose teeth, break out in embarrassing rashes, and if not treated it could kill them!

Soul Pirate Handbook

The Soul Pirate can come down with a nasty case of spiritual scurvy if they aren't feasting on the right things. Your spiritual grub and grog come through spending time with God by reading his story and just talking to him.

Don't get spiritual scurvy.

Bible study is our way to feast on the promises of God.

Just like you have to eat every day to maintain your physical strength, you should feast on God's Word every day to keep your spiritual strength. It keeps the scurvy away. A good place to start is with one of the stories of the adventures of the Pirate King (Matthew, Mark, Luke, or John in the New Testament of the Bible).

Here's a random piratical diet fact: One staple food on board a pirate ship was hardtack biscuits. They were nasty little biscuits that could last for a year. They were said to taste like "digestible leather."

Pirates also ate a lot of pork and turtle! Yup, turtle!
They ate from the galley, which was their version of a school cafeteria. Instead of a lunch lady with a hair net serving up sloppy joes, they had a grumpy pirate with a peg leg serving up salted turtle.

Sea sickness can be a huge problem for pirates too.

Some people get seriously sick anytime they are on a boat. The waves start to roll and they start to hurl. Some people even get sick in the bath tub.

Rather we realize it or not, we all have a serious condition. It's a spiritual sea sickness. It's much more serious than hurling overboard. It is terminal!

We are all sin sick. It will kill us if we don't deal with it, but there is a cure...

"When Jesus returned to Capernaum several days later, the news spread quickly that he was back home. Soon the house where he was staying was so packed with visitors that there was no more room, even outside the door. While he was preaching God's word to them, four men arrived carrying a paralyzed man on a mat. They couldn't bring him to Jesus because of the crowd, so they dug a hole through the roof above his head. Then they lowered the man on his mat, right down in front of Jesus. Seeing their faith, Jesus said to the paralyzed man, 'My child, your sins are forgiven.'

But some of the teachers of religious law who were sitting there thought to themselves, 'What is he saying? This is blasphemy! Only God can forgive sins!'

Jesus knew immediately what they were thinking, so he asked them, 'Why do you question this in your hearts? Is it easier to say to the paralyzed man "Your sins are forgiven," or "Stand up, pick up your mat, and walk"? So I will prove to you that the Son of Man has the authority on earth to forgive sins.' Then Jesus turned to the paralyzed man and said, 'Stand up, pick up your mat, and go home!'

And the man jumped up, grabbed his mat, and walked out through the stunned onlookers. They were all amazed and praised God, exclaiming, 'We've never seen anything like this before!'"
– Mark 2:1-12 (NLT)

I love this story! There is a man who is sick and his sickness has land-locked him.
But he has some friends who are obviously pirates; no one

else would have acted this outrageously! The pirate friends can't get their buddy to Jesus by conventional or comfortable means, so they bring the roof down...literally!
Jesus sees the Soul Pirate faith of the friends and heals the spiritual sea sickness that has paralyzed the man.

The Pirate King heals us from the sickness of our sin.

Set Sail...

- What is one food that you would never try? What is one food that you never want to live without?
- How can a deficiency of God's Word seriously hurt us?
- Have you ever been sea sick?
- What is the cure for spiritual sea sickness?
- What role do the Soul Pirate friends play in their friend's healing? What can we learn from this?

Think on This Soul Piratical Statement

The Soul Pirate can come down with a nasty case of spiritual scurvy if they aren't feasting on the right things.

Navigate the Wild Waters

I'm seriously directionally challenged, I get lost easily! That's why I was amazed a while back when I went out on a boat with a good friend of mine. We left the dock and went for a ride around the lake. We went fast and far. It was beautiful, but honestly, one turn looked just like the last turn. I had no clue where we were. There was no way that I could find my way back to the dock! But after about an hour, my friend found the way back.

He was able to navigate places that I wasn't, because he has some skills that I don't. He has wisdom about the lake, he knows it really well. He grew up on the lake. He knows where to go and where to avoid. He also had a compass, and he knew how to use it. It told him how to go and stay in the right direction.

We've been given navigational tools too. Soul Pirates navigate with wisdom. Soul Pirates navigate with the Fruit of the Spirit.

Soul Pirate Handbook

Soul Pirates navigate with wisdom...

> **"If you need wisdom, ask our generous God, and he will give it to you. He will not rebuke you for asking. But when you ask him, be sure that your faith is in God alone. Do not waver, for a person with divided loyalty is as unsettled as a wave of the sea that is blown and tossed by the wind. Such people should not expect to receive anything from the Lord. Their loyalty is divided between God and the world, and they are unstable in everything they do."**
> **– James 1:5-8 (NLT)**

Wisdom is the ability to live life well and make good decisions. Wisdom doesn't come from old age or hard knocks, wisdom begins with knowing and totally depending on God, who is never stingy to anybody seeking wisdom. We need to get anchored in his wisdom! Wisdom keeps us from getting shipwrecked.

We also get another priceless navigational tool, it's almost an inner compass.

Pirates have to pay attention to a compass, it tells them which direction to go so that they can avoid crashing...that's important! Life can get crazy sometimes.
We can get overwhelmed by waves and we can crash and burn.

It helps if we are paying attention to our spiritual compass. The Fruit of the Spirit is our compass. The fruit needs to be our filter. Our pirate pal Paul said this:

> **"But the Holy Spirit produces this kind of fruit in our lives: love, joy, peace, patience, kindness, goodness, faithfulness, gentleness, and self-control. There is no law against these things!"**
> **– Galatians 5:22-23 (NLT)**

There is no law against these things. There is no penalty when you check yourself with the Fruit of the Spirit, when they are guiding you in directional relationship, and when you use them as a compass for how you act, speak, treat others.

Ask yourself, "Am I operating out of love, joy and peace? Am I patient and kind? Am I good, faithful and gentle? Am I practicing self-control?"

You can avoid a lot of crashes if you are living the Fruit of the Spirit.

Navigate with wisdom and allow the Fruit of the Spirit to be your compass.

That way you always find your way home.

Set Sail...

- Do you have a good sense of direction? Have you ever had to use a compass to find your way? How often do you use a GPS?
- When was the last time you got lost?
- How is wisdom different from knowledge?
- How can we navigate with wisdom?
- How can the Fruit of the Spirit guide you in your relationships?

Think on This Soul Piratical Statement

We've been given navigational tools. Soul Pirates navigate with wisdom. Soul Pirates navigate with the Fruit of the Spirit.

Chapter 25

Step Out of the Boat

Okay, here are some seafaring instructions that don't make sense: The boat is safe and comfortable and familiar, but there will come a time when the Pirate King will ask you to step out of the boat into uncharted places where no one has ever been.

It's scary! You are leaving behind *what* you know to follow *who* you know.
But when you do, you will also discover that spiritual sailing is a skill that the Pirate King always taught by example. He is always out of the boat before we are.

Soul Pirates are not born for normal, we are born for adventure.
Rather than settle, we are ingrained with the need to Step Out!
We find ways to banish boredom.
We long to live unchained and find uncharted places.
We have tasted average, comfort, and control, and we are ready to trade it all in for a whole other world! A world where nobody else has ever walked.

Soul Pirate Handbook

Here's what it looked like for Peter (the patron Saint of Soul Pirates):

> "Immediately after this, Jesus insisted that his disciples get back into the boat and cross to the other side of the lake, while he sent the people home. After sending them home, he went up into the hills by himself to pray. Night fell while he was there alone.
>
> Meanwhile, the disciples were in trouble far away from land, for a strong wind had risen, and they were fighting heavy waves. About three o'clock in the morning Jesus came toward them, walking on the water. When the disciples saw him walking on the water, they were terrified. In their fear, they cried out, 'It's a ghost!'
>
> But Jesus spoke to them at once. 'Don't be afraid,' he said. 'Take courage. I am here!'
>
> Then Peter called to him, 'Lord, if it's really you, tell me to come to you, walking on the water.'
>
> 'Yes, come,' Jesus said.
>
> So Peter went over the side of the boat and walked on the water toward Jesus. But when he saw the strong wind and the waves, he was terrified and began to sink. 'Save me, Lord!' he shouted.
>
> Jesus immediately reached out and grabbed him. 'You have so little faith,' Jesus said. 'Why did you doubt me?'
>
> When they climbed back into the boat, the wind stopped."
>
> – Matthew 14:22-32 (NLT)

There are so many nautical truth nuggets in this story. The Pirate King walked to his crew in the storm. He didn't calm it right away, in fact he invites them to a little water walking party in the midst of the storm. I believe that his invitation was open ended, I think that he was inviting the whole crew to step out of the boat.

Peter was the only one with the guts to get out. The rest of the crew chose to play it safe and stay in the boat.

It's tempting to be a spiritual landlubber. That's someone who lives in the land of comfort and control, but you miss out on the real fun and fundamentally, Soul Pirates want in on the fun.

The Pirate King is walking on the water! Peter sees this as a golden opportunity to do something impossible...he wants in!

Listen in to the conversation...

Peter: "Whoa! Can I play?"
The Pirate King: "*Come*...let's do the impossible."

I like this story because I think it reveals the Pirate King's favorite word: *come*.

We often think that Jesus' favorite word is *go*.
After all didn't he say "*Go* into all the world"?
We get consumed in the *going*. We try to prove our worth by *going* and *doing*.
It's really easy for us to think that Jesus' favorite word is *go*, because that's what we have heard from other authority figures all our lives. "*Go*...get out of here...I'm busy...*go*...leave me alone...*go*...I've had a rough day...leave me alone...*go*."

But Jesus isn't just another authority figure, he is the Pirate King.
And the Pirate King says "*Come*...hang out with me... you belong...I have a place for you...*come*...let's do the impossible together."

He does tell us to go into all the world. But come always precedes go.

Come so that you don't have to *go* alone.
Come so I can give you the Holy Spirit.
Go so that we can do the impossible *together*.
Go, but *come* back often...continually...you are *always welcome*.

Meanwhile, back on the water...the storm is *still* raging. Yet Jesus and Peter are surfing without surfboards! Peter is doing fine as long as he remembers that Jesus said, "Come."

But sadly too often the chaos distracts us from the "come."

Jesus says, "Come," but there is so much to do, we are so busy, we are hurting and confused. Peter was walking on the water until he remembered that he couldn't. He was living in the impossible until he remembered what is possible.
...and he sunk...*glub...glub*.
He was dragged down by the harsh reality of the possible.

Don't get pulled down by what is merely possible.
Thumb your nose at what is possible.
The Pirate King says to us: "Come...let's do the impossible."

Being a Soul Pirate is not for the landlubber or the faint of heart. It's for people who are ready to live curious and courageous.

Make your mark, prepare yourself for amazing sights and incredible adventures all far beyond imagination. Step up, fulfill your destiny, and unleash your pirate soul.

Step out into the uncharted places.

Set Sail...

- Where is a place, which you've never been, that you would love to visit?
- What is something impossible that you would love to do?
- What do you think Peter smelled like?
- Describe the last time that you had to do something that made no sense.
- What does it say to you that sometimes, instead of still-ing the storms, Jesus asks us to step into the storm?

Think on This Soul Piratical Statement

The Pirate King says, "Come...hang out with me...you belong...I have a place for you...come...let's do the impossible together."

Chapter 26

Batten Down the Hatches

Storms can be pretty scary.

I've been in a couple of tornados—they are nasty! It came with a little advance warning…a red faced meteorologist urgently saying something about taking shelter. My survival strategy is usually pretty simple: I sit on the bathroom floor, whimper like a nine-year-old girl and pray hard.

Storms happen.

On a ship, if there was a fierce storm coming, the command would be given to "Batten down the hatches!"

Example:

> "Aye, you scurvy sea dogs, the fierce wind is upon us, you best be battening down the hatches!"
>
> "Aye-aye, Captain!"

This command meant that they needed to prepare for the

Soul Pirate Handbook

storm by fastening down strips of wood (called battens) over all the hatches (the openings).

They had a limited amount of time to brace themselves for the destructive nastiness that was headed their way. Their chances of survival were way higher if the hatches were battened down.

We live on a broken world and bad things happen. That shouldn't surprise us. The Soul Captain told us that it was coming, and he told us to batten down the hatches…

> **"I have told you all this so that you may have peace in me. Here on earth you will have many trials and sorrows. But take heart, because I have overcome the world."**
> **– John 16:33 (NLT)**

That's a promise from God that doesn't get put on many coffee cups or bumper stickers, but maybe it should. It's essential truth for the Soul Pirate.

Brace yourself, batten down the hatches, life is hard. Storms will come. The world can be an ugly place to navigate. **But… don't lose heart! The Pirate King has traveled this way. He is with us in the *now* and the *not yet*.**

Our present life becomes an opportunity to overcome.
Turn trials into traction.
Then…he gives us a cool promise for our *not yet*…

> **"Don't let your hearts be troubled. Trust in God, and trust also in me. There is more than enough room in my Father's home. If this were not so, would I have told you that I am going to prepare a place for you? When everything is ready, I will come and get you, so that you will always be with me where I am. And you know the way to where I am going."**
> **– John 14:1-4 (NLT)**

The Pirate King will someday assemble his entire crew, and that will be an everlasting party!

We prepare for trouble by putting our trust in the Pirate King and staying close to him. He is the author of better days for us.

Bad times come, but we batten down the hatches by constantly reminding ourselves that we are not alone and these problems aren't permanent.
The Pirate King has given us the battens of his peace and his promise.

There is great hope to be found as we sail into the great *not yet*!

Set Sail...

- Have you ever been in a really bad storm? What did you do?
- What does it mean to you that we follow a God who has actually lived on this planet and has experienced troubles like us?
- Describe a time when you became stronger as the result of a trial or troubling time.

Think on This Soul Piratical Statement

The Pirate King has traveled this way. He is with us in the *now* and the *not yet*.

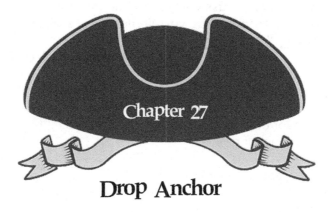

Chapter 27

Drop Anchor

An anchor is essential equipment on a boat. You really should not set sail without it. When you find harbor, you want to drop anchor. It keeps you from drifting away.

The anchor secures a vessel.

The soul is like a restless sailor.
(Yup, I realize that sounds like an 80s pop song).

The currents are always changing; the winds are always blowing.
What are the things that we can make the anchor of our soul?

We need something strong to keep us from drifting.
You want a strong anchor, something that will hold. This is why twisted balloon anchors never really caught on.

"So, God has given both his promise and his oath. These two things are unchangeable because it is impossible for God to lie. Therefore, we who have fled to him for refuge can have great confidence as

we hold to the hope that lies before us. This hope is a strong and trustworthy anchor for our souls. It leads us through the curtain into God's inner sanctuary."

– Hebrews 6:18-19 (NLT)

So, the Soul Captain has given us unchanging anchors that we can cling to, two of those things are his promise and his oath. There are a lot of really cool promises in the Bible, they are unchanging anchor points.

The Soul Captain also gives us his oath. An oath is usually a legal thing. He is swearing to do what he has promised. He backs up *what* he *does* with *who* he is.

That is our anchor.

This gives us hope and harbor. He will do what he has promised. This is like an anchor that steadies our restless souls.

It keeps us from becoming a castaway.

Anchors keep boats grounded. They keep them from drifting when winds, waves, or storms come. God's promise is an unchanging anchor.

Set Sail...

- How important is it to have a strong anchor? Have you ever been in a boat, canoe, or inner tube that drifted away?
- What are some promises in the Bible that have been anchors for you?
- What are some things that try to sway your soul?
- Why is hope a strong and trustworthy anchor in a dark, stormy world?

Think on This Soul Piratical Statement

We need something strong to keep us from drifting. You want a strong anchor, something that will hold. This is why twisted balloon anchors never really caught on.

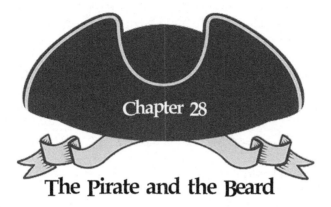

Chapter 28

The Pirate and the Beard

Pirates were big into facial hair. (Even the lady pirates!) It was an essential part of the wardrobe along with a scarf and an eyepatch.

The most famous pirate ever was Black_beard_. (His lesser known brother's name was Beigechin, which is not nearly as intimidating.)

A Soul Pirate can be a lot like a beard.
It's true.
Both a beard and a Soul Pirate can look (or act) a little wild, unruly, crazy.
Sometimes people never get past that.
Sometimes people judge and draw conclusions on *only* what they can see.
Be ready for that!
Excuse me as I climb up on my little soap box...

Except for one misguided week in college, I've had some form of facial hair my entire adult life. It's basically the only thing that prevents me from looking like a chubby 14-year-old boy.

I've experimented with every possible expression of whiskers. I've had full beards in varying lengths, I've sported a goatee, I tried the truck-driver mustache, I have even had a modified Fu Manchu that scared small breeds of dog.

I finally decided to let my chin fruit grow wild and define itself. It has, I believe by divine design, evolved into what I call a "chullet." It is a chin-mullet.

The message is clear: My face is a party.

I think we are living in a golden age for beards. They are everywhere.
They have become a beautiful hairy art form.
Many people celebrate the beauty of the beard.

But there also appears to be a clean-shaven army of beard haters.
Evidently, goatees really get their goat.
They are pretty vocal.
They hate beards and they make that pretty clear.
They spread ugly rumors about the bearded brotherhood.

The latest one has to do with facial feces! A story began to circulate online recently claiming that a "study" assessed the average beards of average men and made a shocking *and* scientific discovery: They are basically dripping with poop! They contend that bearded men are basically carrying around little fuzzy toilets on their faces.

This would really be gross *if it were true!*

I've had several people, including some strangers, feel inclined to show me the study in the last few days. This is basically their way of saying, "Hey, poop face! Have you seen this?" This story has even been reported on several news outlets as actual news.

The thing is...*it's not true!* Turns out that's it's a bunch of...

well...poop.
It's just another blatant attempt by the beard bashers to put
the beard in a box.

It doesn't end online...I have repeatedly been the victim of
facial profiling. I get patted down at every airport I go to,
even when I'm not flying. I've been called homeless, lazy,
uncultured, Gandalf, and Santa. (Come to think of it, those last
two are pretty cool.)

Strangers have told me of their repulsion of my face. I had a
sweet little old lady at church violently grab my chullet and try
to pluck it.

My own mother has expressed her strong dislike for my
chullet. Until recently she would shake her head and say, "You
still have *that* thing!" (So much for having a face only a mother
could love.)

Beard discrimination is real people!

I have a good friend who has a truly epic beard. He keeps it
groomed and properly slathered with beard oil. Some ladies
recently felt it was their moral obligation to make sure that he
is clean shaven. They passed around a petition to make him
shave!

Don't fear the beard.
Don't hate the whiskers.
Clean shaven, stubbled or bearded...
Can't we all just get along?

I have no animosity towards shiny faced men.
They can still be well-constructed Soul Pirates.
If you feel compelled to shave, pick up that razor and go for it!
One of the greatest things about having a face is that you
should be able to do whatever you want with it!
Do whatever you want with your face, I choose to party with
mine.

Soul Pirate Handbook

I can safely say that the chullet is feces free. I shampoo and condition it once a day. Then I apply a magical beard elixir. It is so clean that you could eat off of it, in fact I often do! I don't know why some people hate the beard...could be a phobia or envy. It really doesn't bother me, I'm proud to look like a pirate!

I do have a theory, and here is where this discussion applies to the Soul Pirate...male or female.

Beards look untamed and wild, and some people can't handle that. They like tamed, predictable, and safe. They are freaked out by the facial fuzz.

As a Soul Pirate you are headed into wild, untamed waters.
You will do things that have never been done.
You will be moving from the safe and predictable into the fuzzy and wild.
Don't let the haters on the shore distract you.

Live untamed!

Let the Pirate King clean you up and give you a new name.

But don't let the judgement of the landlubbers trim your sails!

The bottom line is...
Just because something looks untamed doesn't mean that it's unclean.
That's true of beards and it's true of people!
Now, if you don't mind, I've got to go.
I just found a Cheeto in my chullet.

Set Sail...

- Do you currently have a beard? If not, what's your excuse?

- Is there something about your appearance that causes others to unfairly judge you? How did that make you feel?
- Can you remember a time that you judged someone by appearance, and you later realized that you had it all wrong?
- How much courage does it take to be your untamed self?

Think on This Soul Piratical Statement

Just because something looks untamed doesn't mean that it's unclean.

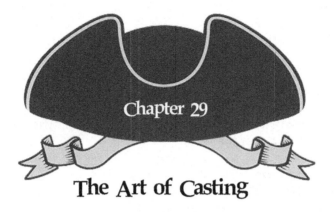

Chapter 29

The Art of Casting

A necessary pirate skill to possess is fishing. We talked about that way back in Chapter 4, but now we are going to examine an entirely different aspect of fishing.

As a man who grew up in the south, it pains me to say it, but I haven't done a lot of fishing in my lifetime. My dad took me a few times until he realized that I really liked to talk. I constantly heard "Shhhh! You will scare the fish away!"

I don't know if that was true...I mean, c'mon, fish don't have ears...right? But if I have to choose between fishing and talking, I'm gonna talk!

I wasn't crazy about baiting my own hook either. Worms are gross. This made my dad doubt that we were even related.

I've got some really cool friends in southern Louisiana who used to take me fishing in the gulf. That was cool! We would stock up on Mountain Dew and snack cakes and go out deep into the bayou. They were very patient with me. They even baited my hook for me...real friends do that! We used huge shrimp as bait. (I always just wanted to forget the fish and fry the bait up.)

I caught a stingray once. That was *awesome.*
I always thought it would be cool to catch fishsticks.

One really important fishing skill that I never mastered was casting.
I mean, c'mon, it's simple…right? You are just throwing your bait or lure out over the water.

I know people who are really good at it.
With a little flick of the wrist, they just let it fly and…*plunk*…it lands exactly where they wanted it to.

That's not me. I'm lucky just to get it in the water. I'm not coordinated and I get easily distracted. Evidently it is good to look where you are casting. I've snagged trees, other boats, and even myself when casting. I fell out of a boat once while trying to cast…I'm not proud of that!

I've never been fly fishing, but I've known a lot of people who really enjoy it.
Casting is an essential skill in fly fishing.

Casting isn't complicated; it's just throwing the bait out. You are casting it away.
But even though it isn't complicated, it is crucial.

That brings us to a Soul Pirate life skill that I'm trying to master: It's casting.
Not casting worms or brightly colored lures.
It's casting cares…burdens…heartaches…failures.
The properly constructed Soul Pirate learns to cast these things away.

I've **got** to learn to cast these things or they **will** sink my boat! The good news is that I've been invited to cast off those things.

I know where to cast, too.

There are some incredibly meaty promises in the Bible about the art of casting:

"Cast all your anxiety on him because he cares for you."
– 1 Peter 5:7

"Cast your troubles upon the Eternal; his care is unceasing!"
– Psalm 55:22 (The Voice)

There are two really cool words in both of those passages: *cast* and *care*.
Let those words bounce around in your boat.

My burdens are too much for me.
My sin.
My failure.
My broken dreams and bruised hopes.
It's too much.
It's too heavy.

The stuff that the culture puts on me…
The stuff that others put on me…
Expectations that I can't live up to…
The disappointments and betrayal of others…
It's too much.
It's too heavy.
My self-inflicted screw-ups.
My temptations.
My troubles.
It's too much.
It's too heavy.

It's good that I don't have to carry it.
I have a place to cast my *crud* because *Christ cares* for me.
My Redeemer promises to be my Rescuer too.

Soul Pirate Handbook

The Pirate King sees my baggage and says, "Throw it here."
That's good because it's killing me to try to carry it by myself.
Often I find that the load that I'm trying to carry is actually
bigger than me.

I am limited. But...he is not.
Nothing is bigger than him.

Don't get weighed down or wiped out.
The infinitely strong One wants to be your burden bearer.
You don't have to carry the load.

Care creates the space for cast.
Look where you are casting...focus on the One who knows you
and loves you and let it fling. With the realization that there
is Someone who cares about you, comes the opportunity to
cast!

Care creates the space for cast.
Sometimes casting isn't pretty. It's sloppy.
It looks like I'm wildly flinging my troubles...that's okay.
It doesn't have to be precise, his arms are big when my aim is
bad.
He promises to catch my problems when I cast them, simply
because he cares for me.

Care creates the space for cast.
Why would I carry what I don't have to?
Your life depends on you learning the art of casting.

Care creates the space for cast.
Stand back I'm about to cast some crud…
Whew!

Set Sail...

- Do you like to fish?
- Do you like to eat fishsticks?

- Can you think of some crud you have been carrying around?
- Are you naturally independent? How is that working for you?
- What does it do to you when you don't cast your anxiety and trouble on the Pirate King?
- Remember that care creates the space for cast and fling it! Practice your casting every day!

Think on This Soul Piratical Statement

I have a place to *cast* my *crud* because *Christ cares* for me.

Chapter 30

Be Strong and Outrageous
Or "Any Respectable Buccaneer
Burns the Blankey"

Outrageous has become one of my favorite words; it's an action-packed word.
It means shocking, unusual, startling, or strange. It is the opposite of normal, quiet, subtle or boring.

It's a fun word that loudly hints that things are about to get inappropriate in all of the most appropriate ways.

I think our faith should be outrageous.
The Bible is an outrageous book!
It's so unbelievable that you just have to believe it!

All through the Bible God asks his people to do outrageous stuff.
Let's look at the slightly crazy story of an Old Testament pirate.
This is the Story of Elisha joining the crew and becoming the first mate of a crusty old seadog named Elijah...

"So Elijah went and found Elisha son of Shaphat plowing a field. There were twelve teams of oxen in the field, and Elisha was plowing with the twelfth

> **team. Elijah went over to him and threw his cloak across his shoulders and then walked away. Elisha left the oxen standing there, ran after Elijah, and said to him, 'First let me go and kiss my father and mother good-bye, and then I will go with you!'**
>
> **Elijah replied, 'Go on back, but think about what I have done to you.'**
>
> **So Elisha returned to his oxen and slaughtered them. He used the wood from the plow to build a fire to roast their flesh. He passed around the meat to the townspeople, and they all ate. Then he went with Elijah as his assistant."**
> **– 1 Kings 19:19-21 (NLT)**

Elijah was an old prophet-pirate who had done some outrageous things. Now it's time to share the adventure. He is looking for a first mate who will take his place.
The Soul Captain directs him to Elisha. Elijah finds him working in a field.

Elisha is plowing a field with two oxen. That's what he does. He plows with oxen. That is his life…it isn't outrageous, it's agricultural. It's what he knows…it's a safe, predictable way to live.

Elijah just walks up to Elisha with a crazy look in his eyes. He didn't say anything. He just threw his nappy bathrobe at him and walked off. Weird, huh? But this was just an invitation to join the big prophecy party. He is symbolically passing his authority to Elisha. He is passing his big pirate hat to him.

Then, in a crazy twist, Elisha destroys what he depended on in the past…his oxen…his security blanket…he literally destroys his old, predictable way of living and doing stuff.

Caution: This is not for the squeamish.

Elisha burns the plow and BBQs the ox.
Suddenly there is no turning back. He can't change his mind about following Elijah, he has eliminated his exit. He is all in.

Outrageous!
This is outrageous obedience! He wastes no time.
He is not playing it safe!
Outrageous!
He left the safe and predictable.
He can't go back to his ox or plow or old way of doing things, it's all gone.

He has burned the blankey because *that* is what buccaneers do!

Soul Pirates live outrageously.

They live with outrageous commitment.
They live in outrageous expectation.
They live because of the most outrageous act of all, God coming to earth to liberate the galley slaves.

Soul Pirate, step away from safe, and step towards outrageousness.

Don't confuse stupid for outrageous.
We were born to do outrageous exploits. Stupid is a cheap, self-centered counterfeit.

Only God can orchestrate outrageous!

The cost of following God is great
The cost of not following God is greater.

Step away from safe and stupid, and step towards outrageousness.
It opens the door for some outrageous stuff!

We think of Elisha as the first mate for Captain Elijah, but his outrageous lifestyle set him up to be a beast! He did more miracles than anyone in the Bible except for Jesus. He did crazy outrageous stuff. He prayed and dead people came back to life, he healed a dude of leprosy, he did a few magical food demonstrations: He multiplied a few loaves of bread to feed an army, and he made some poisonous stew safe. In a truly impressive piratical miracle, he made an axe float.

He was a master of the outrageous!

Some young dudes made fun of him for being bald, and he called down two bears to maul them. The moral to that story: If you mess with baldy, you get the bear!
Even after he died, the outrageous didn't stop! Some raiders threw a dead body into his grave. It touched his bones and *came back to life!*

Outrageous!
But before he walked in outrageous, he had to leave the safe and secure behind.

What is God calling you to leave behind? To burn?
What kinds of outrageousness is God calling you to step into?

We've got to step away from safe and step towards outrageousness.

You probably had a blankey when you were a kid.

You know what I'm talking about, your security blanket. It started life as a warm, fuzzy blanket, maybe with a unicorn or a cartoon pirate. But the years weren't kind to Mr. Blankey. You slept with it, slobbered on it, you drug it everywhere, and the dog chewed on it. It became nappy, smelly, and threadbare. It was falling apart, but you had to have it.

Until...the day when Mom and Dad said it was time. You had to leave it behind. Move on, live without it. Most of the time, by then, it was so toxic that it had to be destroyed.

We grow up, but we still have our security blankets. It could be stuff, fashion, devices, friends, popularity, appearance, or trying to be somebody you are not.

We hang onto those things that make us feel better about ourselves.
The Pirate King wants us to let go of those things and find ourselves in him!

Maybe it's time to symbolically burn the blankey.
Burn the blankey and get outrageous.

Burn the blankey, it cramps your pirate style and swagger.

Step away from safe. Step towards outrageousness.

Be strong and outrageous!

Set Sail...

- What image pops into your Soul Pirate brain when you hear the word outrageous?
- Did you have a blankey when you were a kid? What happened to it?
- What does this statement mean to you: *The cost of following God is great, the cost of not following God is greater?*
- What kinds of outrageousness is God calling you to step into?

Think on This Soul Piratical Statement

Outrageous is a fun word that loudly hints that things are about to get inappropriate in all of the most appropriate ways.

Bonus Soul Booty

A Little Pirate Poetry

Tucked away in the 24th chapter of Luke is one of my favorite Bible stories. It is the story of two heartbroken men walking down a dusty road. Jesus has been crucified and their dreams and expectations have died along with him. They are desperate to pack up their dead dreams and get as far as possible away from the scene of the crime. They just need to sort things out, so they take a walk. They are taking a seven-mile hike from Jerusalem to a crazy little place called Emmaus. They are basically second-string disciples, not Peter or any of the other headliners. They have lived on the fringe of the following, but it seems that God has a real soft spot for the second string...

Suddenly, they are joined by a third man whom they don't recognize. The stranger seems to be clueless about everything that has happened. But then the mystery man tells them that *they* are the ones who need to get a clue. He asks, "Why are your hearts so sluggish?" Then he starts giving them answers. Along with the answers comes recognition...a spark!

This is Jesus! And he is very much *alive*! And he has set their hearts on fire!

> **"They asked each other, 'Were not our hearts burning within us while he talked with us on the road and opened the scriptures to us?'"**
> **– Luke 24:32**

God gives us heartburn! When we spend time with Jesus we are ignited! Sometimes when God shows up we might not recognize him; but, if we walk with him, even accidentally, he will leave us ignited!

He is the source of the heat...
He is the light.
The fire is ignited as we walk and talk with Jesus.

The spark kills the sludge.
Our sluggish hearts come alive.
We are consumed by a holy fire.
Burn, baby, burn!

I also think that is the way that people are meant to find out
about Christ.
We walk alongside them…we talk …our hearts burn…a spark
is ignited.
We are carriers of the flame…
We are the fellowship of the burning heart.
Walk and talk with Jesus! Let him give you heartburn.

I love this story so much that it inspired me to do two things:

1. Get a tattoo
2. Write a poem

The tattoo is on my arm. It's a permanent reminder of the
everlasting flame.

Here's the poem…

"The Fellowship of the Burning Heart"

**I bear on my body the mark…
the mark of the burning heart.**

**Engraved in my skin and engraved still deeper into my
heart is the symbol of the eternal flame.
I have joined the most sacred of orders, the fellowship of
the burning heart.
It is made up of those who have felt their hearts strangely
warmed and failures forgiven.
Those who have touched God and found themselves
forever changed and consumed by an unexplainable fire.**

The broken heart is transformed into the burning heart.

Though at first I didn't recognize him, in time I came to know the Christ as the only one who could set my life aflame.

I have felt the heat of his presence.
Fire is life...
I have been ignited...
I glow in the dark...
I bear on my body the mark...
the mark of the burning heart.

Pirates would shout "Fire in the hole!" before firing a cannon. It was a warning that everything was about to change.

Our Soul Captain has started a fire in our soul and we will never be the same!

Blimey! The Soul Pirate life is not for the squeamish. But ye can do it...

For the King!

> **"Yo ho, all together,**
> **hoist the colors high.**
> **Heave ho, thieves and beggars;**
> **never shall we die."**
> **– Hans Zimmer**

Made in the USA
Monee, IL
28 June 2022

98785067R00090